THE PHILOSOPHY OF

VEGETARIANISM

Daniel A. Dombrowski

The University of Massachusetts Press

Amherst, 1984

Library of Congress Cataloging in Publication Data
Dombrowski, Daniel A.
The philosophy of vegetarianism.
Bibliography: p.
Includes index.
1. Vegetarianism. I. Title.
TX392.D65 1984   613.2′62′01   83-18125
ISBN 0-87023-430-7
ISBN 0-87023-431-5 (pbk.)

CONTENTS

ACKNOWLEDGMENTS

I would like to thank all of the librarians at Saint Joseph's University, the University of Pennsylvania, and Creighton University for helping me locate the material I needed to write this book. I also wish to express gratitude to Mrs. Peggy Troy, a most thorough proofreader, and to the Press's readers of a first draft of this book.

Part of chapter four comes from "Was Plato a Vegetarian?" to appear in *Apeiron*, and part of chapter seven comes from "Rorty on Pre-Linguistic Awareness in Pigs," *Ethics & Animals* 4 (March 1983): 2–5.

1 INTRODUCTION

THE history of ideas is a strange bird indeed. At times, when the Owl of Minerva flies at night, one can detect a steady progress to human thought, which leads some to go so far as to suggest that such progress will inexorably occur in the future. At other times some philosophers of history or historians of philosophy have noticed either a decline in man's reflective ability to deal with the world around him, or a qualitative neutrality in the thought of different ages when these ages are compared. This neutrality may be seen either as a monotonous succession of one theory after another or as a process wherein each intellectual advance is succeeded by a period of barbarism, leaving us with the same human predicament we started with. What is *not* often noticed is the intermittent character of the history of ideas. Often an idea is suggested, held to be true for a while, then ignored, finally to be rediscovered. But if the idea is ignored for too long, the rediscoverers may consider themselves discoverers. This is unfortunate for two reasons: (1) It does an injustice to the original discoverers (or creators) of the idea; and (2), it may prejudiciously result in a too narrowly circumscribed treatment of the idea.

In this book I suggest such an intermittent history to the idea of philosophical vegetarianism, an idea with a history of nearly 1,000 years in ancient Greece. The belief that it is wrong to eat animals was upheld by some of the most prominent ancient philosophers: Pythagoras, Empedocles, Theophrastus, Plutarch, Plotinus, Porphyry, and perhaps even Plato. Then the idea curiously died out for almost seventeen hundred years. After such a long dormancy, all that remained of the idea was ashes, out of which blooms the phoenix of contemporary philosophical vegetarianism. This movement, born in the 1970s, has generated an enormous literature of scholarly books and articles in the most respected philosophy journals. An annotated bibliography of the debate over contemporary philosophical vegetarianism is presented at the end of this volume.

Unfortunately, few scholars attend to the fact that philosophical vegetarianism *is* a phoenixlike presence. Those with the most occlusive blinders think that the issues surrounding this idea were created *ex nihilo*, or perhaps out of the environmental movement of the 1960s. Consider the complete title of Peter Singer's book, the most influential piece in the modern debate: *Animal Liberation: A New Ethics for Our Treatment of Animals*. The curious word in this title is "new," because Singer himself offers a thirty-page summary of the history of philosophical vegetarianism.[1] Michael Fox, who apparently is not a vegetarian and who criticizes Singer, is more on the mark when he says that the controversy regarding vegetarianism is not a new one, but a rekindling of an old one.[2] My point is not to criticize Singer's position; in fact, I largely agree with him. Rather, my hope is to give the contemporary debate some much-needed depth. I plan to accomplish two things through my treatment of Greek philosophy: (1) I will use the tools and insights of the contemporary debate to better understand and criticize the inadequacies of ancient philosophical vegetarianism. And (2), I will use ancient wisdom as an Archimedean point from which I will criticize not only the opponents of contemporary philosophical vegetarianism, but also its defenders. In short, the phoenix I talk of can fly in two directions.

There has been only one lengthy treatment of ancient philosophical vegetarianism, Johannes Haussleiter's *Der Vegetarismus in der antike*. This well-researched work has been invaluable in the development of my treatment of ancient philosophical vegetarianism. However, Haussleiter's work is not the last word on the topic for two reasons: (1) It is inaccessible both to those who do not read German and to those unfamiliar with original manuscripts from antiquity. This eliminates a good portion of those readers who might be interested in his topic. (2) More important, Haussleiter's work is not primarily aimed at isolating the philosophical reasons for the positions held. He treats his topic as antiquarian lore, not as a source for modern debate or insight. He devotes only two pages to the relationship between ancient and modern vegetarianism, and then deals only with superficial facts (e.g., the word "vegetarian" was invented in nineteenth-century England). There is no more indication that Haussleiter could seriously consider the possibility of a vegetarian diet than that he could allow for the diet of the anthropophagist.[3] I will show that philosophical vegetarianism is not a stuffed dinosaur at all, and that the contemporary debate in many ways revitalizes an ancient notion.

What does a contemporary thinker stand to gain from my historical survey? At least three things: (1) To learn about the history of some important issue has an intrinsic worth of its own, quite apart from any refining of contemporary ideas that might occur as a consequence. This is even truer if one learns that there is a history to the issue at all. Philosophers who learn of the historical connections between ancient and contemporary philosophical vegetarianism may naively ask, "Were there vegetarians back then?" Or if they know that there were vegetarians among the ancient philosophers, they often incorrectly claim to know the basis for their vegetarianism. (2) The plurality of assumptions, methods, philosophical anthropologies, and metaphysical beliefs among the ancient vegetarians should make the contemporary philosopher realize that vegetarianism is not a conclusion that follows from any particular assumption, method, philosophical anthropology, or metaphysics. This may also lead one to realize that the split between contemporary vegetarians who are utilitarians (e.g., Peter Singer) and those who are quasi-Kantians (e.g., Tom Regan) is not surprising. And due to the plurality of reasons for ancient vegetarian beliefs, the contemporary opponent to philosophical vegetarianism may come to realize that the position he opposes cannot be dismissed merely as a fad or as a narrow, sectarian position. And (3), one of the approaches in the ancient debate over vegetarianism perceives it as a matter of virtue or excellence (*arete*) rather than, or in addition to, duty. This approach offers the contemporary philosopher a concrete instance of a virtue-based ethics which—at least since Alastair MacIntyre's *After Virtue* (1981)—must be taken seriously as an alternative to utilitarianism and Kantianism. Hints from some of these ancient vegetarians may help contemporary philosophers, vegetarian or not, understand the nature of a virtue-based ethics. I will return to this theme again in chapter 7.

Chapters 2 through 6 explore the phoenix of philosophical vegetarianism, i.e., philosophical vegetarianism in ancient Greece and in the contemporary debate. It will unfold that ancient vegetarians had several bases for their stance: (1) a mythological belief in a past vegetarian golden age; (2) a faith in transmigration, which led them to spare animals in the belief that animals were, or would become, human beings; (3) a concern that flesh-eating was injurious to the health of either body or soul—the former being tied to ancient medical thought, and the latter concern associated with a more general commitment to moderation or asceticism. But it will also be seen that (4) there was among the ancients a concern for animals themselves —inasmuch as animals either suffer before they are killed or are deprived of their life even if killed painlessly, and in that we can lead healthy lives on vegetal food, eating meat is cruel and ought to be avoided. This fourth foundation for vegetarianism includes what are now called the arguments from sentiency and marginal cases. The rest of this chapter, however, deals with the ashes. Why did the phoenix die? What kept it dead for so long? What forces have allowed the bird to become reconstituted? These are the questions I am concerned with at present. I must announce at the outset that I will be dealing exclusively with Western philosophy. In the East, or in parts of it, vegetarianism has been not a phoenix but a Methusele over two millenia old.[4] So the more precise question is, Why did the phoenix die in the West? Initially the answer seems to lie squarely on the lap of Judeo-Christian tradition. Eventually I will qualify this position.

In Genesis 1:24–28, we are told that God made man in His own image. Using Feuerbach's notion that if birds could theologize, God would have feathers, we can ask whether it is man, the meat eater, who creates God in his image. Because man is said to have been made in God's image, and nonhuman animals were not, man was given dominion over every living thing, a dominion that includes killing and eating animals. After the Fall, God himself clothed Adam and Eve in animal skins (Genesis 3:21); thus we should not be surprised when men offer God animal sacrifices in return for His goodness.[5] This reciprocation, naturally enough, puts the fear of God *and* man into animals (Genesis 9:1–3). It is true that men were given some guidance regarding animals; for example, they were not to boil a kid in its mother's milk (Exodus 23:19). But this offers no solace to the kid, who could presumably be boiled nonetheless. It is also true that Isaiah predicted a time when the lion would dwell with the lamb; unfortunately, there is no clear indication that the lamb could dwell peacefully with man. In short, the Hebrews viewed man as the crown of creation, a status which denigrates animals.

Asses and oxen were valuable as property, however. Perhaps this is why Jesus allows one to pull an animal out of a pit, even on the Sabbath (Luke 14:5). The New Testament seems to leave animals in the same situation as the Old. Jesus himself showed indifference (if not cruelty) to nonhumans when he unnecessarily forced 2,000 swine to hurl themselves into the sea (Matthew 5:1–13). St. Paul asked with scorn, Does God care for oxen? Of course not (I Corinthians 9:9–10)!

As Singer notices, the example given by Jesus was not lost on later Christians. St. Augustine thought that to refrain from killing animals was the height of superstition, and that we need not behave toward animals as we do toward men.[6] Neither we nor God need care about animals. The aforementioned kid, the one not to be boiled in its mother's milk, becomes a symbol for Christ.[7] Symbols, property, inferior pieces of creation meant for man: such are animals for St. Augustine. This attitude is somewhat understandable in that the Manichees were vegetarians, and St. Augustine, himself a Manichee for over a decade, wanted to divorce himself from this part of his past. He was also correct in suggesting that the vegetarianism of the Manichees was little else than superstition. The elect, they believed, could extract spiritual power from eating plants (and even here only under special conditions) but not from animals. But in the course of attacking the Manichees, St. Augustine developed a general attitude about man's treatment of animals. After considering the swine that Jesus forced into the sea, St. Augustine even suggested that animal *suffering* meant little or nothing to human beings. (We will see this position come back to haunt St. Augustine and others.) In a final rationalization, animals are disassociated from us because of their lack of reason.[8]

The general rule in the Judeo-Christian tradition is not without exceptions. Ecclesiastes 3:19 suggests that man and beast share one breath—whatever that means in the context of the boiling kid. St. John Chrysostom suggested that saints should extend their gentleness even to unreasoning creatures.[9] Why only saints should be so gentle is unclear. Basil the Great composed a prayer for animals in which he suggests that God saves both man and beast. And, of course, there is St. Francis of Assisi. But as Passmore notes, his case is not a clear one.[10] His *Canticle to the Sun*, in which he "preaches" to the birds, is an attempt to exhort the birds to glorify God. Although St. Francis is often perceived as a syrupy nature lover, or at least as a Christian who did not think that nature had to be dominated, he did not prohibit his followers from eating meat. When he did prohibit meat, it was during times of fasting for ascetic reasons rather than out of concern for animals. Seen in this light, St. Francis is one of the more famous "animal lovers" who showed his love by eating them! [11] One cannot help but notice the anomaly involved when these same individuals are called "people lovers." But St. Francis would never have thought of cannibalism, for he, along with this tradition in general, saw man made in the image of God. The following quote regarding St. Francis's love of nature is instructive:

> While this kind of ecstatic universal love can be a wonderful fountain of compassion and goodness, the lack of rational reflection can also do much to counteract its beneficial consequences. If we love rocks, trees, plants, larks, and oxen equally, we may lose sight of the essential differences between them, most importantly, the differences in degree of sentience. We may then think that since we have to eat to survive, and since we cannot eat without killing something we love, it does not matter which we kill. Possibly it was for this reason that St. Francis's love for birds and oxen appears not to have led him to cease eating them; and when he drew up the rules for the conduct of the friars in the order he founded, he gave no instruction that they were to abstain from meat, except on certain feast days. [12]

What the Christian position needs above all else is a rational justification. As with so many other topics, the intellectual framework supporting the Christian view of animals is best exhibited in the writings of St. Thomas Aquinas. In the *Summa Contra Gentiles* St. Thomas tries to provide some metaphysical support for the theological belief in man's dominion over animals, which is due to another sort of dominion: the control man has over his actions, a control animals lack. [13] That is, human beings are self-movers, whereas animals are mere instruments existing for the good of man, presumably because they are not self-movers. Because the intellectual nature alone is free, animals are naturally slaves due to the fact that they are not rational. Intellectual creatures hold the highest place in the universe because, except for the angels, they approach nearest to the divine likeness. Therefore, St. Thomas concludes, *all* others are for the sake of man (my emphasis).

Although St. Thomas goes into more depth on this issue than any other medieval thinker, not even he really argues his case; his theological background (and perhaps his Aristotelianism) made argument unnecessary. Six points come to mind regarding this text: (1) Given St. Thomas's contention that animals have no control over their actions, one wonders what he would say about the practice of chastising a dog that has relieved himself where he was not supposed to. (2) One could ask what *does* cause an animal to "move" (if not himself) in a way that does not similarly "move" human beings. St. Thomas gives little, if any, indication. To reply with "nature" or "instinct" is to beg the question, inasmuch as human beings are also natural beings with instincts; indeed, they are animals themselves.[14] (3) It is not at all clear that animals completely lack rationality, as we shall see later. In any event, St. Thomas does not show that they lack rationality. (4) Even if human beings do approach nearest to the divine likeness, it does not follow that all beings "beneath" man are for his sake. (5) There is quite a gap between suggesting that a being that lacks freedom and rationality—assuming for the moment that animals lack these—is therefore a slave or a mere instrument. And (6), because St. Thomas was wrong about the natural slavery of some human beings—a realization that Christians never fully grasped until the nineteenth century—one might be led to question whether the natural inferiority of animals is as intuitively or theologically obvious as St. Thomas thinks.

In this same passage St. Thomas finds himself in a bind of sorts. When he contends that it is not wrong for man to make use of animals, either by killing or in *any* other way (my emphasis, but not my point), his ideas seem to conflict with some scriptural passages that forbid us to be cruel to animals, e.g., not to kill a bird with its young. St. Thomas's "solution" is ingenious, and remained popular long after the Middle Ages: it is wrong to be cruel to animals not because of the pain inflicted on the animals, but because it may lead one to be cruel to human beings.[15] I will leave untouched the question as to whether this is what scripture intends, although it is hard to imagine how prohibiting us from boiling a kid in its mother's milk is meant to prevent us from boiling a human being in *its* mother's (or anyone's) milk. Rather, I will now introduce one of the key terms from the modern debate: *speciesism*. This term refers to the attitude which allows the interests of one's own species to override the sometimes greater interests of other species. The term seems to have been invented by Richard Ryder, but was popularized by Peter Singer.[16] I introduce this term to make an accusation: the Judeo-Christian tradition, even as exercised by a sophisticated thinker like St. Thomas, has been speciesist. As I will argue later, even if animals are not rational (which St. Thomas never proves), and even if human beings do most closely approximate the divine likeness, there is no reason to infer that animals are our slaves and can be treated in any way whatsoever, as long as our treatment of them does not lead to cruelty to human beings. The issue of slavery is not raised here as a histrionic show. Just as racism and sexism were once (and still are?) accepted in even the most intelligent circles, but were then unmasked for their obvious injustices, so might the same have occurred for speciesism. The point is that just as Plato glimpsed the evils of sexism in Book Five of the *Republic*, so did many Greek thinkers glimpse, or in a few cases clearly view, the evils of speciesism.

What often amazes the philosophical vegetarian about the speciesist is, of all things, his naiveté. St. Thomas blindly assumes that it is necessary to eat meat.[17] Although he may legitimately condemn Manichean thought along with St. Augustine, what reason does he have to suspect the health of the Manichees? Naiveté may not be a fault, but a lack of charity is, especially for a Christian. God loves animals because he loves all things that are (Wisdom 11:25). Yet human beings could not be charitable to animals even if they wanted to, for three reasons: (1) Charity is a kind of friendship, and we wish good for our friends, but animals are not capable of possessing good. (2) Friendship is based on fellowship, e.g., living together, and no animal can enter into fellowship with a human being. And (3), charity is based on the fellowship of everlasting happiness, which animals cannot obtain.[18]

Once again, I must counter these assertions: (1) It is not clear why we cannot condescend to show charity to animals when even God can; it should be remembered that Jesus commended his Father for caring even for the fall of a sparrow (Matthew 10:28).[19] (2) St. Thomas does not show why having the ability to possess good (a fuzzy notion which is left unexplained) is necessary for one to be shown charity. The whole point to Christian *agape*, as opposed to passionate *eros*, is that it is a love which does not demand love in return. Or, in Povilitis's language, there is no reason to conclude that the golden rule entails a mutual obligation.[20] (3) Some animals *do* show fellowship to human beings, e.g., pets. And (4), it is not readily apparent why charity can be given only to those capable of eternal life.

If my criticisms of the Christian attitude toward animals seem harsh it is because familiarity breeds annoyance, if not contempt. There is no reason why Christianity had to take the course it did regarding animals. When hearts are given over to enslavement instead of to sharing our goods with animals, or at least to acting as stewards to God's bounty, it is hard to see how one has not violated the law of *agape*. Stephen R. L. Clark and Andrew Linzey perform a service for Christianity by suggesting that the orthodox should be castigated for inventing a war against the beasts in order to gain a sense of their own identity as human beings made in God's image.[21] If I understand *agape* correctly, one need not subjugate other beings, much less eat them, in order to earn a dignified place in God's eye. But it is St. Thomas's view—not Clark's, or even St. Francis's ideal— that held sway at least until the mid-nineteenth century, when Pope Pius IX refused to allow a SPCA to be established in Rome on the grounds that to do so would imply that human beings have duties toward animals.[22]

I am examining three segments within the period of ashes. With the end of the first segment at the close of the Middle Ages, one might suspect that, due to man's belief that he was specially made in God's image, the attack on animals would cease. This is hardly the case. Animals remained in a state of servitude long after man literally believed in Genesis. As Singer notes, Renaissance humanism was, after all, *humanism*, a term that has little to do with acting humanely.[23] The source of Renaissance denigration of animals lay not only in Christianity, but also in a return to the ancients; specifically, a return to the Protagorean dictum, "Man is the measure of all things." Although this insistence on the value of humanity advanced the situation of human beings, it left nonhumans in the same sad state they had occupied at least since the Middle Ages. Renaissance writers like Pico della Mirandola prided themselves on being more worthy of admiration—because they were human—than anything else in the world. Some dissenters can be found: Leonardo da Vinci became a vegetarian because of his concern for the suffering of animals, and Montaigne's favorite author was the ancient vegetarian Plutarch (see chapter 5). Generally speaking, however, with respect to animals, man's central place in the universe remained in a pre-Copernican state long after Copernicus wrote. Yet this gets us ahead of the story a bit. The absolute nadir comes in the thought of Descartes.

All are familiar with Descartes's dualism of mind and body; it is not unfair to say that Descartes regarded animals as mere bodies. In *Discourse on Method* he refers to animals as automata or moving machines. The only apparent difference between machines and animals is that the latter are made by God, who is a better machine-maker than we are. Two criteria are needed to show that a being is not merely a machine: (1) speech, which puts thought on record, and (2) reason. Animals lack these criteria. Descartes even goes so far as to suggest that next to those who deny God, the most powerful agents attempting to lead us away from virtue are those who suggest that animals share man's nature. These people—and apparently Descartes has some unnamed ancients in mind—are suggesting that we have nothing more to fear and hope for than the flies and ants.[24]

Speciesism has never been exhibited more clearly, and for five reasons: (1) Descartes *assumes* that animals are automata made by God. One might expect the patient analysis Descartes exhibits elsewhere, for example, in the first meditation, but none can be found here. (2) As with St. Thomas, Descartes does not argue that animals lack reason; with the weight of speciesist thought behind him, no argument is thought to be needed. (3) To suggest a continuum in animal psychology, including beasts and man, is not, as Descartes implies, the same as saying that animals have the same nature as man. (4) Nor does the "unity of psychology" commit one to the Kafka-like dread of a life of an insect.[25] (5) Finally, Descartes's treatment of language is question-begging. This last point will now be treated in some detail, as it will reappear in the writings of some contemporary analysts, including Rorty (see chapter 7).

Descartes contends that animals cannot possess language because they do not have our anatomical structure. (They do, but insofar as this is a detailed empirical question, I will pass it over to others more competent.) When confronted with monkeys and parrots, which at least seem to speak, Descartes immediately counters that this is not real speech but a material disposition similar to the workings of a clock.[26] One wonders how many human beings would have to be declared automata if judged by the same criteria, given the fact that most men are not mathematicians who fully understand statements like *cogito ergo sum*.

By suggesting that animals are automata Descartes is not only denying animals rationality, but is also denying consciousness itself. In a way, he must be admired for his consistency here. As long as thinkers like St. Thomas admit that animals can feel pain, it *would* be cruel to inflict pain on them unnecessarily. *If* this is Descartes's insight, he seems to be right on the mark. But from this insight Descartes feels compelled to arrive at one of the most incredible conclusions in the history of philosophy: animals do not feel pain. This belief comfortably allowed Descartes and his followers at Port Royal not only to eat meat but also to engage in vivesection with impunity: "They nailed the poor animals up on boards by their four paws to vivesect them and see the circulation of the blood."[27]

Descartes would admit that animals seem to experience pain, but because they cannot speak to us about this pain they must not have it. But it is not at all clear that linguistic ability is the sort of evidence that allows us to infer pain in a human being, especially in babies.[28] Once again, why such stringent criteria in the case of animals?

The situation changes somewhat in Descartes's letters. In a letter to the Marquess of Newcastle, he supplies the only evidence of the nonrationality of animals which does not beg the question: animals imitate or surpass us only in those of our actions which are not guided by our thoughts.[29] This surely will not do because even if what Descartes says is true, it does not follow that animals are completely devoid of reason. And in a letter to Henry More, Descartes admits that just because he does not have an argument to show that animals think, it does not follow that they do not think.[30] He also admits that it seems likely that animals experience sensation like us. It is passages like these that allow Cottingham to come to the defense of Descartes.[31] Cottingham contends that Descartes does not hold the monstrous view of animals that some would suggest, inasmuch as Descartes does, at points, concede that animals have sensation. However, even Cottingham admits that Descartes's position is by no means consistent. For example, in this same letter to More, Descartes reaffirms his belief that animals would tell us of their thoughts *if* they had any. Descartes concludes that those who suspect a crime in the killing of animals are continuing the superstitions of Pythagoras. (I will consider Pythagoras in chapter 3.)

Who is being superstitious here? The question is, why does Descartes sustain the speciesist position to the extent that he does? It may well be that blind adherence to tradition, if not superstition, is at work. Passmore notices that in his attitude toward animals, Descartes is at least tangentially treating a theological problem.[32] The problem is how to account for the apparent suffering of animals in a world governed by God. St. Augustine solved the problem by saying that there is a lesson for human beings in animal suffering.[33] Malebranche quite explicitly (and Descartes implicitly) solved the problem by suggesting that because suffering is the result of Adam's sin, and inasmuch as animals are not descended from Adam, animals do not suffer. I would hold, however, that theological neatness and the need for a carte blanche to do vivesection are not sufficient reasons to draw the conclusions Descartes draws.

Another major figure in this second segment of the period of ashes is Kant, who was anything but a callous man. Yet in his *Lectures on Ethics* he sees animals only as a means to man's end.[34] Although we can ask, Why do animals exist? (for man, of course!), the question, Why does man exist? is meaningless. This double standard should be familiar by now. Remember, in the *Grundlegung* one of the formulations of the categorical imperative reads: "Act in such a way that you always treat *humanity* . . ." (my emphasis).

Kant, however, does not totally denigrate animals. Their nature is analogous to human nature, a point Descartes would not grant. And the more we come into contact with animals, the more we love them, which shows more generosity than St. Thomas was able to exhibit.[35] Kant even goes so far as to suggest that there must be a reason why humane people do not destroy animals, leading him to praise some unnamed Greek thinkers. Again, as in the case of St. Thomas, Kant never suspects that this insight contains within it the foundations for philosophical vegetarianism. Kant *assumes* we need meat.

Do we have duties to animals? An excellent study on Kant by Broadie and Pybus explores this issue.[36] There are two sorts of duties in question: (1) direct duties *to* something; and (2) indirect duties *with regard* to something. An example of the latter would be returning a borrowed book in good condition to a friend. The direct duty is toward the friend. We have indirect duties toward animals which, if fulfilled, help us support our direct duties to human beings. Like St. Thomas, Kant believes that he who is cruel to animals is also hard in his dealings with men. The fact that this is an empirical claim in need of verification does not seem to have been realized by Kant. Passmore notes that the converse may not be true: tyrants from Nero to Himmler have been notoriously devoted to animals.[37]

It may well be, as Broadie and Pybus claim, that in addition to his Christianity, another source of Kant's treatment of animals is his rationalism.[38] By emphasizing a peculiar sort of human reason, Kant fails to do justice to the role that the capacity for suffering plays in determining moral duties. In fairness to Kant it should be noted that in his thought there is a complex relationship between ends in themselves, on the one hand, and beings who are capable of recognizing the moral law, are autonomous, and can participate in the moral community of the Kantian "kingdom of ends," on the other hand. One is tempted to ask why we should not exclude nonrational human beings from the scope of moral concern: infants, the mentally defective, and so on. I will treat this (Kantian) problem when I come to the argument from marginal cases in chapter 5.

Might it be the case, however, that the key question to ask Kant is, Could there be anything morally intermediate between persons (ends in themselves) and stones (mere means)?[39] If we can love an animal (as Kant thinks we can), and not a stone or a book, might there not be degrees of indirect duties, if not direct duties? How can one love a mere thing? If humane persons ought not to be cruel to animals, whereas the issue of cruelty is not applicable to mere things, why does Kant think of animals only as means?

The second and third segments in the period of ashes overlap. The third segment started at least as far back as the Renaissance, and the second segment continues in certain ways up to the present. The second segment perpetuated the medieval view of animals long after the Middle Ages was over. The third segment can be called the "era of excuses."[40] In this segment we find thinkers who no longer accept the Judeo-Christian account of animals, have come to the brink of philosophical vegetarianism, and then fall back into the safe domain of traditional gastronomy. Not all have had a failure of nerve. As I mentioned, Leonardo da Vinci must have realized the implications of the

decline of the medieval version of man's dominion when he became a vegetarian, but he was not a philosopher who left us a
detailed position.

The list of those who came close to doing what Leonardo did
is long, and can only be examined cursorily here, but the reader
should get the drift of this third segment. Montaigne was skeptical of human claims to superiority over animals, and said that
"presumption is our natural and original disease." Yet he was
not a vegetarian. Voltaire criticized Descartes and his Port Royal
followers: "Answer me, machinist, has nature arranged all the
means of feeling in this animal, so that it may not feel?" Yet he
ate animals. Rousseau seems to have recognized the strength of
the arguments for vegetarianism without adopting the practice.
Seidler shows how Hume was led to a consideration of animals
by (1) the skeptical tradition of Montaigne-Bayle, (2) his own
experimental method derived from Newton, and (3) ethical
considerations. Although Hume admits that animals are capable
of passion and reason, he feels they lack a moral sense, so our
ethics do not extend to them. It is remarkable how close these
thinkers came to philosophical vegetarianism, but still fell
short of it. Schopenhauer criticized Kant's position on animals,
using Eastern ideas in his critique; yet he consoles himself with
the following soporific device: "Without animal food the human race could not even exist *in the North*" (my emphasis).[41]

In late eighteenth- and nineteenth-century British thought,
the era of excuses picks up steam. This is due to the fact that it
is in this period that we find two seminal thinkers who realize
why animals deserve our respect, yet who fail to consistently
follow their own arguments to their logical conclusions. First
came Jeremy Bentham, who posed a question that has become a
commonplace in the contemporary debate: "The question is
not, Can they *reason?* nor Can they *talk?* but Can they *suffer?*"[42]
After Bentham included animals within the utilitarian calculus, however, he wished them speedily killed (to soften the
blow, of course) in order to eat them. I will return to utilitarianism later. Suffice it to note here a point that Nozick makes: *If*
experiences of pleasure, pain, and so on, are morally relevant,

then animals must be counted in moral calculations to the extent that they *do* have these capacities and experiences.[43]

The second figure is Charles Darwin, whose position in many ways is the normative one today. He explicitly holds, as anyone must hold who understands the theory of evolution, that "there is no fundamental difference between man and the higher mammals."[44] Animals feel pain, love, have the desire to be loved, suffer from ennui, have dreams, possess the ability to reason and remember, and for all we know, may be self-conscious as well as conscious. Although animals do not have the ennobling belief in God, many human beings do not have this belief either (nor do some men have reason), and we do not (or should not) kill and eat *them*. In short, Darwin thinks, the golden rule should be applied to animals.

As Singer emphasizes, once the weight of evidence in favor of Darwin's theory became apparent, practically every earlier justification of man's supreme place in creation and his dominion over the animals had to be rejected. Darwin signals a revolution in our perception of animals: we *are* animals! Although Darwin demolished the intellectual framework of speciesism, he retained in his own personal life many speciesist practices, including eating meat. Singer puts it well: "It is a distinctive characteristic of an ideology that it resists refutation."[45]

This introductory chapter is not intended as a comprehensive view of the history of philosophers' views on animals. I have mentioned the above figures only to provide an informed background against which to consider the issues with which the ancients dealt, and to furnish a sense of the obstacles these thinkers must overcome if they are to be taken seriously today. In many ways the contemporary debate is a contest between the post-Darwin excuse-makers and the neo-Hellenizers (who may also pay a debt to Darwin).[46] One purpose of this book is to make this latter position self-conscious of its Greek foundations.

2 THE GOLDEN AGE

THERE was a pervasive sense in ancient Greek culture that the past was better than the present. At times this belief conjured a golden age of perfection in which vegetarianism was practiced. It is this belief that is the subject of this chapter. Although these "once upon a time" stories of a contract between man and animal are merely stories, so are the "once upon a time" stories of a contract between man and man.[1] In that this condition has not bothered the history of social contract theory from Plato to Kant to Rawls, it should not bother us. That is, these stories of an ancient vegetarian past, even if not true, offer insight into the beliefs of the people who told them.

The two key elements in understanding the ancient vegetarian age are the myth of the ages and the story of Prometheus.[2] These two elements are often depicted in conflict, with degeneration away from the golden age being the point of the myth of the ages, and progress from original primitivism being the point of the Prometheus story. In the case of vegetarianism, however, the Prometheus story also has a pessimistic ring.

The best place to start a discussion of the golden age is with Hesiod's *Works and Days* (109–201). This passage establishes that the first race of men, the golden race, was created by the gods of Olympus, who were ruled by Cronus. This race eventually became regarded as inhabitants of a golden age because of the happiness of their existence. They were free from sorrow, toil, grief, and evil. Death for them was nothing more than going to sleep, which itself hardly seemed necessary in that they did not have to work so they never got tired. It is important to note that these men did not even have to work for food, as they were fed out of a boundless cornucopia. Because the fecund earth spontaneously bore them abundant fruit (*karpon*), they could live in ease and peace on the land *with* their flocks. (Elsewhere Hesiod suggests that in this age the gods and men ate their meals in common, a practice that loomed large both in Spartan ways and in Plato's thought.)[3] Cultural primitivism does not even enter into Hesiod's account of the golden age; the implication seems to be that the simple (i.e., vegetarian) life is best.

The golden age—the age of Cronus—eventually yields, through force, to rule under Zeus. A new race of silver men comes on the scene, not as descendants of the golden race, but as a new creation. This race was foolish and inclined toward insolence—e.g., they did not sacrifice on the holy altars of the gods. Such impiety led Zeus to destroy this mentally and physically inferior race. Zeus created a third race, that of bronze, out of ash trees. Although it is not clear if they were worse than the silver race, they must have been at least as bad because they took a delight in violence. In this age might made right, and eventually men destroyed each other, namelessly descending to Hades. It is significant to note that this race did not eat bread, even if we do not know what they did eat. Because this race was a physically violent one, we can let our imaginations wander.

The fourth race signals a respite, for it is not designated by a metal, but is called the age of heroes. Although these demigods also died in battle, they were rewarded for their virtue by being sent to the Islands of the Blessed, where Cronus rules over them in glory. Part of the honor of their fate is that the earth bears honeyed fruit for them, a signal of a return to the golden age.

The fifth race, the age of iron, continues on the temporarily interrupted path of degeneration. Toil, anxiety, sorrow, war, and *hybris* characterize this age. This is apparently the worst of races, and the one Hesiod identifies with, leading to his desire to have been born before or after this age in the belief that the golden age will perhaps return. No doubt one expression of man's *hybris* in this age was his attitude toward animals.

Although the first explicit reference to the myth of the ages was made by Hesiod in the eighth century, it seems that Homer implies such a schema in indirect ways. In the *Iliad* (I, 260–68) Nestor talks of the better men who preceded him; and as Haussleiter notes, the Olympians of ancient times themselves ate ambrosia and nectar. In Homer's day meat was still a rarity, a sacred meal.[4] Further, the most monstrous character in Homer's corpus, the Cyclops Polyphemus, engaged in anthropophagy, the culinary habit most removed from pristine vegetarianism.[5] However, in the *Odyssey* (IX, 105–565) we learn that although the land of the Cyclops was itself wild and untamed, a kind of golden age prevailed: there was no need to plow or hunt because the land produced on its own. As a matter of fact, it can be said that it is Odysseus and his men who provoke bloodshed, for it is only because of their desire to steal cheeses that bloodshed against human beings (not animals) starts.

It is after Hesiod, however, that the legacy of the myth of the ages becomes apparent. In the fifth century Empedocles holds that ancient man was better than contemporary man because of the former's vegetarianism and because of the absence of war and animal sacrifices.[6] Although Empedocles does not explicitly identify the men of this former age as inhabitants of the golden age, the similarities are clear. These men offered to their deity things like statues, pictures, perfumes, and honey. They did not offer animals because, as Empedocles says, to kill an animal for food or sacrifice is the greatest abomination among men! At another point he says that these men were gentle to each other *and* to animals and birds.[7] Porphyry's *De abstinentia*, a work to be treated in detail later, makes it clear that Empedocles was making a plea for vegetarianism (II, 20–21). If men were dominated by Love (*Cypris*) they would be vegetarian; but in an age of Hate, or in an age at least partially dominated by Hate, killing animals is a natural consequence.[8] Empedocles' portrayal of man's once-amiable relations with animals becomes a matter of literary tradition for Greek culture, and eventually finds its way into the writings of Alexander Pope.[9]

In terms of conceptual richness Plato more ably treats the myth of the golden age than any other thinker. As early as the *Gorgias* (523A, 523C) Plato explores the difference between the age of Cronus and the age of Zeus. But many passages suggest that Plato did not view the first men as a golden race in a paradisiacal state.[10] Therefore, Plato's use of these ages must be in order to make a philosophical rather than a historical point. A preliminary example comes from the *Republic* (415A). He who is fit to rule—the philosopher—has some gold in him; the guardians are to be of silver stock; whereas bronze and iron are found in the producing class. (It is interesting to note that none of the three classes in the *Republic* is of heroic blood.) If Plato does not believe that Hesiod's ages are true historic accounts, why does he allude to them? It seems he uses them not as history, but as exemplifications of what *would* have happened had any of these groups ruled. Complete peace and moral progress are only possible in a golden age, i.e., an age dominated by philosophers.

It is highly doubtful that Plato thinks such an age could actually exist, because this golden generation was not autonomous; it was determined by the decrees of Cronus. But according to Hesiod, when the ages of Zeus are ushered in (the silver generation on), human beings determine their own fate. Thus, an age dominated by guardian types (silver) would be one of recklessness, due to a lack of control from the rational part of the soul. Even worse would be a stage of history in which power would be in the hands of the producers (bronze, iron), for in such an age the dominant leitmotif would be the identification of justice with force. Thus, in a metaphorical way, Plato could be said to agree with Hesiod that the present age was one of iron. If this interpretation of this part of the *Republic* (415) is correct, then the whole work can be viewed as if Plato is imagining that stage in history as ruled by those who were golden, like the gods. This interpretation does justice not only to this passage, but also to Book Two where the ideal city is first mentioned (369C). This passage makes it clear that the Republic is a created city whose real creator is the needs of people living in an age of iron (also 423A).

How does this relate to the issue of vegetarianism? Plato believed that at least some of the ancients were vegetarians, as we learn through the speech of the Athenian in the *Laws* (782). The question is whether Plato's peculiar belief in "golden boys" corresponds to his awareness of vegetarianism. The needed connection is found in the *Statesman* (269–74), in the famous myth of cosmic reversal. Here it is stated that those men living in the age of Cronus were vegetarians. This link will enable me to unravel much in Plato's attitude toward man and beast.

Plato's reversal myth goes as follows: There is an era in which god (*theos*) himself guides the universe and gives it rotation, and an era in which he (i.e., Cronus) releases his control. In this latter era the world revolves under its own influence, a circumstance made possible by the fact that god has endowed it with reason. The Eleatic Stranger's description of the age of Cronus is somewhat familiar by now: All good things came without man's labor. Man did not even have to plan or govern the universe. Tutelary deities or a *daemon* did that for him by acting as shepherds to a flock. Savagery was nowhere to be found, nor preying of creature on creature; no strife existed. Men had fruit without stint from trees and bushes; these needed no cultivation but sprang up of themselves out of the ground. This pastoral life even meant sleeping on the soft bed of grass offered up by the earth. The communion among animal species was such that human beings conversed not only with each other, but also with animals, seeking to learn what they could about the special faculties human beings lacked. Although it is not clear if these partners actually engaged in dialectic, the Eleatic Stranger makes it clear that they *could* have.

When this order of things came to its destined end, universal change was ushered in. Cronus and his regional deities withdrew their hands from the earth's rudder, and destiny (*heimarmene*) took control of the world again. The shock of reversal in the world's processes resulted in the destruction of living creatures, followed by a period of recovery. After this period of solace, the world ruled itself. At first it remembered the instruction it had received from god, but gradually its memory grew dim due to its bodily element. Whereas the world receives its order from god, it is also permeated by the chaotic and disorderly force of its bodily factor.

When, in this age of Zeus, the primacy of god (i.e., Cronus) is forgotten, chaos gradually asserts itself. Plato makes it clear that his age is subject to the regency of Zeus. Bereft of the guardianship of Cronus's helpers, man became weak and helpless and was ravaged by wild beasts (perhaps because he could no longer communicate with them). Even previously friendly beasts turned savage, indicating that the change was not just an alteration in human nature. The earth no longer supplied food spontaneously, and poor man lacked any knowledge or tools to cultivate the soil. Let me leave man in this terrible predicament for just a moment to make two inferences:

(1) Philosophers should be vegetarians. This conclusion can be drawn when the story of the ages in the *Republic* (where Plato is imagining what history would be like if golden types-philosophers ruled) is joined with the evidence of the *Statesman* (that those in the golden race under Cronus are vegetarians). (2) Vegetarianism seems to be an unreachable goal, however, because the point to the myth of cosmic reversal in the *Statesman* is that the ideal universe under Cronus has never existed in the physical realm any more than the Republic has.[11] This is not to say that vegetarian thought is not useful; it does supply the ideal background against which to judge our treatment of animals, in the same way that the Republic provides the paradigm against which judgments of actually existing historical states are to be made. The consequences of this separation of paradigm and *praxis* will be considered in chapter 4.

Plato's use of myth in the *Statesman* takes us to the heart of the issue of vegetarianism in Greek philosophy. As Vidal-Naquet has noticed, this myth is really Plato's clever merger of three logically distinct myths: the myth of planetary reversal; the myth of the earthborn (the gegeneis); and the myth of a golden age under Cronus.[12] He also observes that the last part of the overall myth—that dealing with Cronus—is treated in the *Republic* (378A) with great care because it can easily be distorted (presumably by those who would needlessly raise romantic hopes). Vidal-Naquet contends, rightly I think, that the paradise of the golden age was primarily an animal paradise. The pastoral vocabulary of the age under Cronus is replaced by a political vocabulary under Zeus.

Returning to the age of Zeus, man was in a pitiable state of deprivation, obviously the historical condition that Plato thought man was originally in, insofar as the golden age is an ideal construction (or reality) that never really existed in *this* world.[13] It was in order to meet man's needs that Plato introduces the gifts of the gods Hephaestus and Prometheus. They gave man fire (which is also a symbol for mind), craftsmanship, and other tools to help him fend for himself.[14] Prometheus, the very god who was responsible for the status of social man, was also the god who furnished fire for cooking and who was responsible for the break with animals (and gods?).[15] Prometheus's gift of fire ensures the transition from the golden age to the human ages under Zeus, for fire cooks a meat eater's diet. Although this diet allowed man to survive when his lot was less than sanguine, it also severed man's friendly link with animals.

Interestingly, it is the ambiguity of Prometheus's character that helps clarify the function of the myth of the golden age of vegetarianism. From Vidal-Naquet's point of view, the "age of Cronus" is a slogan for philosophical and religious sects not satisfied with the existing civic order. Relying on Detienne, Vidal-Naquet holds that this situation calls for some sort of cultural transcendence, which can proceed in two directions.[16] In the upward direction an attempt is made to implant in "our" world the vegetarian virtues of the golden age—which is what Pythagoras, Empedocles, Porphyry, and others tried to do. In the downward direction an effort could be made to contact bestiality through a Dionysian type of consumption of raw food, which in its extreme form could lead to cannibalism.

These two directions are no strangers to our age. Our countless "natural" products and the practice of vegetarianism are both examples of "upward transcendence," whereas back-to-nature movements that shun baths and cleanliness are examples of "downward transcendence."[17] Although my gaze will be primarily upward in this book, a brief glance down at some of the Cynics seems appropriate at this point.

It is fitting that the founder of this sect, Antisthenes, was not a full-fledged Athenian, but a bastard. The lifestyle of the Cynics was based on a deliberate transgression of all conventions, especially those dealing with diet and sex.[18] They often ate their food raw, and masturbated in public. It is not accidental that Antisthenes wrote two treatises on the Cyclops, and that Diogenes wrote one on Thyestes, who unwittingly ate his own children. Nor is it surprising that the Cynic version of the age of Cronus did not necessarily include vegetarianism. Insofar as some Cynics were, paradoxically, vegetarians, one might infer that both varieties of transcendence are two sides of one unnatural coin.[19] Later I will show that such is not the case. I would argue that the cynical exception proves the rule. When the Greeks (including Plato) imagined a perfect life, they generally imagined a life in communion with the animals, a life in which man did not "have" to eat flesh. Perhaps modern scientific studies of the healthiness of a vegetarian diet would have persuaded these Greeks that they did not "have" to do what they often did.

Before we leave Plato, one more point should be discussed. In the *Laws* (713), the Athenian draws an analogy between Cronus's daemons and the men they ruled, on the one hand, and human shepherds and the animals they tend, on the other. The point to be made is that dominion is not a license for eating. It would be unfathomable for Cronus's helpers to eat men just because they were superior in intelligence. The lesson for human dominion seems clear enough, yet often curiously missed (see *Republic* [342–343]).

Aristotle does not discuss vegetarianism in ancient times, but his student Theophrastus does.[20] For Theophrastus, grass was the most ancient sort of sacrifice to the gods, followed by trees, which led to the saying "enough of the oak" when fruits, barley, frankincense, and so on, replaced tree leaves. Only later did man sacrifice animals, an act which defiled religion, according to Theophrastus, who was a vegetarian.

Our understanding of vegetarianism in the golden age is greatly enhanced by the little-known Dicaerchus of the late fourth century, whose *Life in Greece* (*Bios tes Hellados*) is preserved in part by Porphyry.[21] Because Dicaerchus, like Theophrastus, was a Peripatetic, it is apparent that vegetarianism made quite a mark on Aristotle's followers, if not on Aristotle himself. I will show later that there is good reason for the Peripatetics to be interested in this issue. For Dicaerchus, the golden race never killed animals, a notion that he takes from the long-dead Hesiod (*Works and Days*, 116): men did not have to work, for they ate foods that possessed a cathartic power, which was believed to be the key to health.

Because the golden age was one of abundance, a person from the greedy iron age might suspect that the golden age was an age of opulence. The opposite was true. The golden race was characterized by frugality and simple eating. Its members could afford to be frugal because with an overflow of food on hand, there was no great desire to be a glutton.[22] The moderation of the golden race also allowed them to live in peace. This ideal life was followed by a pastoral period when men initially only meddled with animals. They tamed the malefic and attacked the savage. The attack was concomitant with the origin of war, illustrating the unity of the war psychology.[23] The third form of life, the agricultural, eventually led to a complacent concern for property and the desire to obtain more than others.

As Lovejoy and Boas notice, Dicaerchus's *Life in Greece* is the first cultural history of a people; but Dicaerchus is original for other reasons as well.[24] When the Pythagoreans are considered I will note that many assume that the Greeks were vegetarians primarily because of the prevalent belief in transmigration of souls. Dicaerchus, however, was a materialist Peripatetic who denied not only the immortality, but also the existence of the soul.[25] Thus, his fascination with vegetarianism seems to stem from what can be called the unity of animal psychology, including human psychology.[26] Linking animal eating with war clearly shows that Dicaerchus perceives ancient vegetarian man as superior, because of his belief that it is morally wrong to inflict unnecessary suffering on a being that can experience pain. Finally, although Dicaerchus's name is not familiar to us, he was a favorite among many of the ancients, e.g., Plutarch and Cicero.[27]

Another rarely mentioned fourth-century writer is the historian Ephorus. He brings into sharp relief the notion that present day "noble savages" are persistent remnants of the golden age.[28] That is, the idealized barbarian is the myth of the golden age stripped of any chronological ties; Plato's philosophical treatment of the golden age certainly prepared the way for this innovation. Ephorus's portrayal of the vegetarian Scythians and their meat-eating neighbors (including the Greeks) does not represent succession in time but contiguity in space.[29] By describing the Scythians as vegetarians, Ephorus is distinguishing them for their justice and their simplicity of life. Although the Scythians lived far away, Ephorus was said to have actually visited them in an attempt to be empirically accurate.

Ephorus's explicitness, however, should not blind us to the same ideas Homer implied in the happy lands, far, far away, i.e., the golden age surviving in odd corners of the world. The Ethiopians to the south, the Hyperboreans and Thulians to the north, and the Islands of the Blessed to the west are cases in point. In fact, it seems fair to say that the qualities attributed to the mythological Hyperboreans are transferred by Ephorus to the not wholly unknown Scythians.[30]

In the third century the Stoic poet Aratus puts a few new wrinkles in Hesiod's myth of the ages.[31] The golden age remains pretty much the same: men lived simple vegetarian lives in peace, and they did use animals, albeit humanely, by allowing the ox to pull a plow. By the bronze age, however, the evil-working sword they had forged was used to kill the ox in order to eat it; working *on* the ox instead of working *with* him. In his consistent moral tone, or moralizing, Aratus shows a heavier hand than Hesiod. And each generation he portrays is born of the previous one—as opposed to the fresh creations of Hesiod —thereby suggesting that the discontinuation of the vegetarian life was at least partly due to poor education, a matter that would not apply as much in Hesiod's model. The effect of education on culinary habits is still an interesting issue. Most of us were taught that a balanced meal is located on a tripartite plate for meat, potato, and vegetable. Perhaps this is why even some philosophers and classicists cannot take the issue of vegetarianism seriously. When they think of a vegetarian they imagine a poor fellow whose platter is one-third empty! [32]

In the first century B.C., Diodorus Siculus wrote a prefix to his universal history of the world in which he offers a brief account of the genesis of the world.[33] Peculiar to this account, influenced by Epicurean sources, is the merger of the golden age with the myth of the earthborn, but in a different combination than Plato's. Although the first men were undisciplined and brutish, they were vegetarians nonetheless. However, they were attacked by wild beasts, indicating that the rift between man and beast is not primarily due to man or to Prometheus's gifts, but to the animals. Yet man was no darling, for he entered groups established for the mutual safety of the members solely out of self-interest.[34] As history progressed man learned how to cope better with the natural world. The first men, who were vegetarians, were not in a blissful state; they were miserable. Whereas previous versions of the myth regarded man's ignorance of agriculture as a positive sign that this bounteous earth could sustain him without such knowledge, here such ignorance is a negative condition illustrated by those who died in winter because of a lack of food. When they became acquainted with fire (through Prometheus) they could ameliorate the less-

than-desirable features of their existence by cooking and stor-
ing foods.

What is noteworthy in Diodorus Siculus's account is that he
is the first to negatively view primitive vegetarianism and the
golden age; what is praised is technical progress in the domination of nature.[35] One might suspect at this point that the Greeks
had finally overcome their enchantment with the golden age
and its vegetarianism, and had opened their eyes to the new
dawn of "common sense." Hardly. I believe that vegetarianism
was always controversial in Greek culture, constantly influenced by the intellectual and political climate of the day.

The moral tone of Aratus is maintained by Ovid in his *Metamorphoses*. This Roman writer—whose life spanned the first
centuries of both eras—alleges that man is superior to the other
animals because of his lofty thought and a countenance turned
toward the stars, as opposed to the other animals who looked
downward.[36] In the words of Genesis, man had dominion. Yet
man's rule over the earth was not totalitarian. He cherished
righteousness in the golden age; not only did he not engage in
war with animals or other men, he did not strip the mountains
of trees. This illustrates that Ovid's description of ancient vegetarianism was tied to a more complete ecological frame of mind.
Callicott reminds us, as does Ovid, that animal liberation can be
a closed-minded affair if it *completely* excludes consideration
of plants, soils, and waters, even if the latter do not possess sentiency.[37] Ovid portrays the earth of the golden age as untouched
by hoe and unwounded by plow, as giving all things freely. This
romantic (and unfounded) faith in virgin soil is often connected with primeval vegetarianism, as Passmore has noted.[38]
Ovid's gods yield acorns, fruits, and berries in an eternal spring
where the placid Zephyrs gently cool the honey and the flowers.

Once again one can see how the ancient mind equated pacifism and juristic primitivism, on the one hand, and vegetarianism, on the other. When the silver race appeared, however, me-
teorological "wars" brought both fiery heat and icicles, creating
the need to preserve grain by felling it with a sickle; once the
friendly tie to plants had been lost, only animals remained to be

yoked, which eventually occurred in the groans of bullocks. The last race, that of iron, appeared to be better than Ovid's own, which followed the iron race. Although the iron race was replete with trickery, avarice, bellicosity, and the killing of animals, and although it saw the rape of mother earth with unnatural boundary lines to demarcate private property, it at least spared the trees, an omission that did not escape Ovid's own day.

Ovid's image of gentle Zephyr wrapping its fingers around honeyed oaks may be too much for less romantic moderns to bear, but it should be noted that this scenario was also a bit too much for some ancients. In the poem *Aetna* (9–16), which legend ascribes to Virgil, the golden age is satirized:

> Who does not know of the Golden Age, of the king who was free from care, when no one sowed wheat in the plowed fields or kept weeds out of the future crops, but brimming harvests yearly filled the granaries? The wine pressed itself and honey dripped from sticky leaves and Pallas caused mysterious rivers of fat olive oil to flow. Then was the time of rural charm. No one could know his own age better than this.[39]

That fact that we do know our own age better than one with sticky leaves and self-pressing grapes indicates the major flaw of imaginative, rather than philosophical, vegetarianism: its frivolity.

Plato and Plotinus force us nonetheless to take the myth seriously. Inasmuch as the latter was himself a vegetarian, this is all the more significant. The quest for unity is at the center of his thought—and will be treated in more depth later. But here I want to attend to the fact that Plotinus's concern for the One includes plants and animals, references to which abound in the *Enneads*. In fact, in various places Plotinus calls on the myth of the ages and all it connotes to illustrate the "architecture of the universe."[40] The One (*to hen*) is "symbolized" by Ouranos, the transcendent heaven which is not really amenable to predication or cognition. The intelligible realm of divine intellect, however, is knowable and properly symbolized by the golden age of Cronus, "son" of Ouranos. All in this realm is immortal, divine, and intelligent, which presumably includes the vegetarianism of the golden age. The very name Cronus suggests exuberance (koros) and intellect (nous). Cronus engendered Zeus, who symbolizes soul (psyche) instead of intellect. Thus, Zeus reigns over the besouled world of animals that longs for its "father" and "grandfather," for the establishment of real being, and for salvation itself. Cronus is thus sandwiched between two realms. Because he is fettered to an unchanging identity, he leaves to his "son" the task of ordering the universe. Trying to ignore this world, Cronus strives for the higher world of his "father." Because Zeus is pulled by the material world (hyle) beneath him, his striving for the One is even more difficult than Cronus's, and can only be accomplished by imitating the degree of perfection found in his "father's" golden age. Seen in this light, vegetarianism is hardly frivolous or inaccessible, but is instead an easily reached rung on a ladder that climbs to that unity which is much more difficult to attain.

Plotinus's pupil, Porphyry, was also a vegetarian who made allusions to the golden age. He seems to believe that before men sacrificed animals to the gods, they abstained altogether from animal food (De abstinentia II, 10). Furthermore, he sees the degeneration away from the golden age as gradual. After men started to slay animals they still spared those that cooperated with man in works beneficial to him (II, 31). Continuing the Pythagorean tradition he quotes Empedocles:

> Ah me, while yet exempt from such a crime,
> Why was I not destroyed by cruel Time,
> Before these lips began the guilty deed,
> On the dire nutriment of flesh to feed? [II, 31]

Unfortunately for Porphyry, human exemption from eating animal flesh was temporally finite; the degeneration continued until a certain point in history when it reached its logical (although not necessary) conclusion: eating human flesh (II, 53). As we will see later, Porphyry's response to these varying degrees of carnivorousness is to vicariously return to an age of true freedom and justice where, as he quotes Hesiod, "The fertile earth for them spontaneously yields / Abundantly her fruits" (III, 27).

What can be gained from a consideration of all of these treatments of the golden age? Some would say nothing, because of the paucity of proper philosophical argument. Without being overly generous in applying the principle of charity, I think that there is something very important at work here. The notion of labor is a helpful heuristic to get at the heart of the thought considered in this chapter. For Hesiod, what made the golden age so blissful was the absence of labor and the need for it. When the transition was made to the ages under Zeus, labor was needed, or—as Diodorus Siculus pointed out—man would starve. This is why Prometheus is so important: he (along with Hephaestus) symbolized successful work and intelligent craftsmanship. The reactions to this world of labor in large part determined attitudes toward vegetarianism. On the one hand Promethean *praxis* was necessary for survival, yet on the other hand there was a desire to escape from labor and a concern for utility. Or better, the Greeks wanted not so much to escape from labor but rather from the bland utilitarian view of the world that labor fosters. This attitude is illustrated in Plato's conception of rule by the producing class as the least desirable (i.e., it is this class which gives rise to the tyrant); in Dicaerchus's denigration of a too zealous concern for property; and in Ovid's citation of landowners' boundary lines as an indication of decadence. Even Plotinus's identification of Zeus, *psyche*, and energy metaphorically indicates how far removed labor is from primal bliss.

This opposition between Promethean praxis and the golden age provides a challenge to the contemporary philosophical scene, in that we feel the Greek tension far less acutely. At least since Bacon and Descartes laid the intellectual foundations of the modern world, we have largely been content with the Promethean view through our equation of technology and industry with progress. Our current behavior toward animals is in many ways the antithesis of the golden age. An animal's nature is determined solely by the utilitarian value we see in, and bestow

upon, him.[41] We classify objects as edible or inedible and guar-
antee the immutability of this distinction by taking all potential
edibles and making them into absolute edibles. Other objects—
e.g., fine china—acquire status to the extent that they enhance
the status of the edibles. This anthropocentric order is built totally upon a utilitarian (i.e., Promethean) base. If this anthropocentrism can be proved inadequate, then myths concerning the
golden age may not be as quaint and antediluvian as they first
seem. In short, Feuerbach's notion may have to be bestowed with
a new intellectual coinage: in a way, man is what he eats, not
just in a trivial sense, but in the more profound sense that when
man gets hungry he springs into action, especially through labor. These actions, in turn, often determine the values we place
on nonhumans without our ever being consciously aware of the
process by which these values are formed. But in a bastardized
way we still cherish at least one of the values of the golden
age: getting the most output for the least work—hence factory
farming.[42]

3 THE PYTHAGOREANS

ACOMFORTABLE transition can be made at this point to the thought of Pythagoras. This sixth-century figure was born into a milieu which for centuries had been permeated by vegetarian ideals. Pythagoras's genius is that he gave these ideals some sort of philosophical foundation. Tom Regan rightly suggests that Pythagoras is the father of philosophical vegetarianism.[1] But Pythagoras certainly did not initiate the attempt to recapture the golden age by abstaining from animal food.

At least two important prephilosophical movements introduced Pythagoras to vegetarianism. The Orphics were a mystical cult that practiced vegetarianism, but for unknown reasons. Their motivation was probably connected to their belief in the transmigration of souls. Animals were animated with souls that would eventually be, or had previously been, found in a human body. Orpheus himself was believed to have had the power to move animals with his voice. Because it was also believed that he had the same power over plants and rocks, some problems arise with a vegetarianism built solely on the basis of transmigration. If plants are as besouled as animals, what are we to eat? Although Pythagorean vegetarianism overcame these problems, the similarity between the Orphic and Pythagorean cults cannot be denied. In fact, the religious communities founded by Pythagoras were modeled after the Orphic communities in Greece and Italy.[2] The other major influence on Pythagoras's vegetarianism was the priestly class in Egypt. We learn from Herodotus that the Egyptians were the first to develop the notion of transmigration of souls from terrestrial, to marine, to avicular life, and finally to a human body.[3] Thus, presumably for the same reasons as the Orphics—who may have copied the Egyptians—these priests abstained from eating meat and fish. And, strangely enough, they refused to eat beans.[4] All this sounds like primitive taboo. If these are Pythagoras's sources, how can he escape Descartes's charge that his vegetarianism is merely a matter of superstition? And how can a philosopher like Regan defend Pythagorean beliefs?[5] The road to an adequate philosophical defense of vegetarianism will be an arduous one. What makes a philosophical approach difficult is the fact that the Pythagoreans were, like the Egyptian priests, largely a secret society concerned with ritual purity, even down to the linen (not woolen) clothes they wore.[6] This is a far cry from Socrates' open dialectic in the agora.

There are scholarly problems as well. Despite the fact that there has been as much preserved about Pythagoras as about any figure in antiquity, we still have great difficulty knowing who he was. Nothing remains of anything he may have written. The reports about him from late antiquity, upon which I must largely rely, are in conflict, and later Pythagoreans, who existed centuries after the master, are understandably open to the charge of distortion or hyperbole. Therefore, my treatment will have to be tentative and evenhanded, constantly weighing one interpretation against the other.

It seems that Pythagoras spent his early years on the island of Samos, and eventually went to Asia Minor where he was exposed to the thought of Thales and Anaximander.[7] From Thales he could have learned that the entire universe was animated (i.e., "full of gods"); this panpsychism, as I suggested, could lead one to vegetarianism (and beyond). He could have adopted

Anaximander's crude notion of evolution and changed it into the psychic migration for which the Pythagoreans became famous. From Asia Minor, there is some indication that Pythagoras went to Egypt and Babylon. Here he could have made contact not only with the aforementioned priests, but also with both Far Eastern thought (and its vegetarianism?) and Zoroastrian ideas, which also prohibited eating meat and beans.[8] After these travels it appears that Pythagoras tried to settle down. But only after several false starts and exiles did he establish his society in Magna Graecia, or contemporary Italy. It is at this stage that any knowledge about Pythagoras himself is to be found. I will first deal with the agreed-upon elements regarding Pythagoras's vegetarianism, reserving the more controversial (and interesting) hypotheses for the end of the chapter.

Pythagoras's name has been linked with vegetarianism since the century after his death, to Juvenal, to Plutarch, to Diogenes Laertius and Porphyry, to Voltaire, and the contemporary debate.[9] This vegetarianism is supported by three foundations: (1) religious beliefs, including transmigration; (2) reasons of health; and (3) ethical considerations.

(1) Pythagoras was so sure of transmigration that he even admitted his own preexistence.[10] Furthermore, through rites of purification, including abstinence from meat, one could remember previous lives.[11] This cyclicism indicates that nothing is absolutely new, although it is only through ascetical eating practices that one can learn this. The following quote from Porphyry gives us the most detailed picture not only of Pythagoras's general diet, but also of its ascetical modifications when he sacrificed to the gods:

> Of his diet, the breakfast was honeycomb or honey, the dinner bread of millet or barley and vegetables, whether boiled or raw. He would eat only rarely of the flesh of sacrificial victims, and this not from every part of the body. Generally, when he was about to descend into adyta (shrines) of the gods and remain there for some time, he used foods that

would keep away hunger and thirst. That which would keep away hunger he composed of poppy seed and sesame and the skin of a squill (an herb) washed carefully until cleansed of the juice around it, and flower stalks of asphodel, and leaves of mallow and barley groats and barley corns and chick peas, all of which he chopped up in equal quantities and soaked the choppings with honey from Hymettus. That which would keep away thirst he made of cucumber seeds and juicy raisins, from which he took out the seeds, and coriander flowers and seed of mallow (again) and purslane (another herb) and cheese gratings and the finest wheat meal and cream, all of which he mixed with honey from the islands. He said Hercules had learned these recipes from Demeter when he was sent into waterless Libya. . . . In sacrificing to the gods he practiced simplicity, propitiating them with barley groats and a cake and frankincense and myrtles, and occasionally with cocks and with the tenderest of pigs. He once sacrificed an ox, however (but according to the more accurate authorities, it was an ox made of dough), when he found the square of the hypotenuse of a right triangle equal to the sum of squares of the other sides.[12]

Iamblichus's account essentially agrees that Pythagoras sacrificed cakes, honey, and frankincense to the gods.[13] The only time Pythagoras ate meat was when the gods demanded it, and this was rare. As regards those foods and drinks that keep hunger away, Gorman is instructive:

It was usual for the Greeks about to undergo initiation to eat such a mixture, which was in fact the sacred "kykeon" of the mysteries at Eleusis. The opium poppy was sacred to the goddess Demeter whose statues always appear crowned with them; the poppy was not only used to banish hunger and produce a feeling of well-being in the darkness and mystery of the caves and shrines of the gods, but also produced a state of acute wakefulness for up to eight hours as well as visual hallucinations which prepared the initiate for the arrival of the gods. In its last stages the poppy causes a mystical state between waking and sleeping when bizarre phantasms, both visual and aural, begin to manifest themselves. The initiate would then fall into a dream after the trance-like state of the preceding hours. It was in the dream that the god made his epiphany or appearance to the initiate. This was the usual procedure in the temples of the god of healing, Asclepius, whose devotees received cures in their sleep. The properties of the ancient squill are unknown, but may have been another narcotic to produce endurance in the face of the fears in the dark. However, the most important ingredient in the mixture mentioned by Porphyry first was the opium poppy.[14]

Later, Porphyry explains which animal parts were always prohibited, even in sacrifice: (1) the testes and genitals—referred to as the *beginning* of an animal—for without them no animal would come into being; (2) the brain, because it was the cause of *increase* in all growth; (3) the feet, which were the *source* of movement; and (4) the head—referred to as the *end* of the animal—due to its great administrative power.[15]

Diogenes Laertius gives even more details, but offers a picture similar to Porphyry's.[16] Pythagoras forbade above all else red mullet, blacktail, and gurnard (types of fish); the hearts and bellies of animals (for unstated reasons); and beans (to be treated later). He did content himself, nonetheless, with honey or a honeycomb, and bread; he never touched wine, at least not in the daytime. Apparently he liked boiled or raw greens, and every once in a while some fish. Although Diogenes Laertius does not say so, there must have been some religious compulsion for the latter—as we will soon see in an upcoming fish tale. Pythagoras's offerings were always inanimate (*apsychois*); Diogenes Laertius has little faith in those accounts which suggest that Pythagoras offered cocks, goats, porkers, or lambs. He approvingly quotes Mnesimachus, Aristophon, and Heraclides, respectively:

> To Loxias we sacrifice: Pythagoras his rite,
> Of nothing that is animate we ever take a bite.
>
> Their food is just greens, and to wet it pure
>   water is all that they drink.
>
> So wise was wise Pythagoras that he
> Would touch no meats, but called it impious,
> Bade others eat. Good wisdom: not for us
> To do the wrong; let others impious be.

It is also made clear by Diogenes Laertius that vegetarianism was a matter of purificational catharsis for Pythagoras, and catharsis entailed the avoidance of birth and death. Avoidance of birth, in turn, entailed the avoidance of eggs and egg-sprung animals.[17]

It should not be concluded at this early juncture, as Singer seems to do, that Pythagoras was a vegetarian *only* because of his belief in ritual and transmigration.[18] Yet we can see why Singer might reach this conclusion when one considers all of the apocryphal stories concerning Pythagoras. The most famous is the tale about Pythagoras when he stopped a man from beating a dog because he recognized in the dog the voice of an old friend.[19] Iamblichus supplies us with some other winners among Pythagoras's dicta: do not kill a flea (especially in a temple!), and do not clean your teeth with a myrtle leaf.[20] Such pronouncements help us understand why Shakespeare has Malvolio reject the opinion of the Clown (i.e., Pythagoras) in *Twelfth Night* that to kill a woodcock would be to dispossess the soul of his grandmother.[21] Even in antiquity Claudius the Neopolitan thought that Pythagoras was insane.[22] Without doubting Pythagoras's sanity, one must admit that in some respects he seems to have been a Manichee before his time, whose purity included not only abstinence from meat but also the avoidance of any contact with cooks or hunters.[23]

The incredible tales go on. Pythagoras, in Christ-like fashion, was a miracle worker with animals. Whereas Jesus performed a miracle so fishermen could *eat* fish (Luke 5 : 1 – 11), Pythagoras performed a miracle to *save* the fish.[24] The story goes that Pythagoras once happened upon fishermen drawing in a great catch, and bet that he could predict the exact number of fish in the nets. When he did precisely this he won his wish: to let the fish go alive, as none had died yet. The irony is that Pythagoras claimed himself to be a fisherman in a previous life.[25] He also forbade the destruction of animals, except the most noxious ones—e.g., he is said to have bitten a poisonous snake to death! His friendliness to animals makes him even more akin to St. Francis (or is it the other way around?) than Jesus: he pet an eagle, told an ox to avoid trampling on beans (to the amazement of the oxherd), and fed the Daunian bear barley and acorns, admonishing it to attack no longer. Evidently the bear obeyed, despite having previously wounded several inhabitants of the region.[26] From the Pythagorean perspective, however, these events are not really miracles but expressions of the fact that all of these animals are besouled (*empsychon*).[27] This stretches the modern mind a bit, to say the least, especially when the story of the fishermen is considered. How could besouled fish enable Pythagoras to count them?

Not all animals are equally ensouled for Pythagoras—for several reasons to be discussed later. Of prime importance here are the special relationships some animals have with the gods. Among the sacred animals were white cocks, which were never to be sacrificed because they were sacred to the sun or to some other astronomical phenomenon.[28] Pythagoras's dislike of bloody sacrifice led him to revere the bloodless altar at Delos.[29] Diogenes Laertius tells us that Pythagoras offered flour, meal, and cakes at Delos without the use of fire. The bloodless nature of this shrine is even attested to by Aristotle, we are told, in his *Constitution of Delos*.[30] Pythagoras also found reading the entrails of beasts anathema. This does not mean that he was opposed to all forms of augury, as he did see omens in the flights of birds, rather than in the ripping apart of their chests.[31]

Now we come to the second of the three foundations supporting Pythagoras's vegetarianism. (2) He did not regard vegetarianism as only a religious matter; he also was a proponent of the "victory through vegetables" hypothesis,[32] which suggests that a vegetarian life is healthier than a meat-eating one. Although Pythagoras's life is variously reported to have been between 70 and 104 years, his longevity was usually ascribed to his having eaten certain plants and to his extensive medical knowledge.[33] Once again, Porphyry is most helpful:

> As a result of this diet Pythagoras kept his body always in the same condition, as if in a scale. He was not sometimes healthy and sometimes sick, nor again sometimes getting fatter and increasing in girth, sometimes losing weight and thinning down. His soul, too, always revealed through his appearance the same disposition, for he was neither much relaxed by pleasure nor withdrawn because of pain, nor did he ever seem to be in the grip of joy or grief; indeed, no one ever saw him either laughing or weeping.[34]

One can see here a closer connection than might be expected between body (*soma*) and soul (*psyche*). As Rorty emphasized, the Greek concept of soul developed out of Homer's notion of the soul as a shadow of the body.[35] The rigid dualism of "the ghost in the machine" is a Cartesian notion that only partially relies on Christianity for its support; it relies even less on "dualistic" Greek thinkers like Pythagoras and Plato. Here we should notice the conception that Porphyry attributes to Pythagoras, in which soul and body function as an integral unit, unlike the extrinsic mechanism (from the point of view of the soul) of Descartes's pineal gland. Bodily disposition and psychic disposition are inextricably linked. The old dictum raises its head again: you are what you eat. Pythagoras had a great variety of foods to eat, including a plethora of fruits and roots. All of these foods affect our attitudes, beliefs, and spiritual condition. Those who pay no mind to these connections may be rudely awakened to their effect after ingesting fermented grapes.[36] That is, eating meat is an intoxication in its own right. Pythagoras's abstinence from wine and meat (or at least his temperance regarding the former) may explain why he was never reportedly doubled over in peals of laughter. According to Diogenes Laertius, the real reason Pythagoras forbade an animal diet was to accustom his followers to such a simple life that they could sustain themselves on easily procurable, raw foods.[37] This diet, along with only the purest drinking water (cf., the Perrier craze), was the way to a healthy body (*somatos hygieian*) *and* mind.

Pythagoras obviously appreciated the necessity—even the pleasure—of food, as is indicated in the story of his being made weak by a forced fasting on a long sailing voyage. His asceticism was not exactly the stern sort later exemplified by Christian monks in the deserts of Egypt. He only seems to "preach" a type of temperance. Because this moderation entails abstinence from meat and wine, and a paucity of food according to Iamblichus, we modern gluttons tend to lump Pythagoras together with all other proponents of self-control and/or self-denial of food.[38]

An apparent contradiction arises when considering the athletic life. Although vegetarianism is regarded as a source of health and longevity, Porphyry reported that Pythagoras advised the Samian athlete Eurymenes to eat meat so as to defeat his cheese and fig-eating opponent in the Olympics.[39] This report makes it clear, however, that Pythagoras eventually regretted giving this advice, most likely because of the atavistic attitudes and jealousies that meat-eating engenders. The fact that Eurymenes won his match still leaves Porphyry unresolved about the question of bodily health. Perhaps Diogenes Laertius and Iamblichus were right that Eurymenes' trainer was not Pythagoras the philosopher at all, but another man with the same name.[40]

I will now turn to the fascinating subject of beans. Inasmuch as the Pythagoreans opted to worship the gods with plants rather than with animals, it should not be surprising that some plants were considered sacred. For example, the oak was sacred to Zeus. In addition, statues resembling parts of the cosmos (*agalmata*—see the above quote from Porphyry, which refers to an ox figure made from dough) were offered, but not until they were covered with laurel, rue (an herb), poppy, or marjoram. Beans are thus only one category of sacred plant. If they are especially sacred it is because they arose from the primordial slime at the same time as man.[41] Diogenes Laertius refers to Aristotle's work *On the Pythagoreans*, where it is held that Pythagoras counseled abstinence from beans for various reasons: they are like genitals (i.e., the beginning of things), or the gates of Hades, or the number one (because they are unjointed), or the universe as a whole, or because they belong to an oligarchy (in that they were used as counting devices in an election by lot).[42] You can take your pick of bean images.

Pythagoras may have borrowed the notion of primordial slime and the importance of water either from Thales or the Egyptians. According to Porphyry, this slime was the rotted putrefaction of the source of things—the golden age?—which had been thrown into confusion. The supposed affinity between man and bean was thus "proven" by Pythagoras: he put beans in a pot and buried them in mud; when he dug them up ninety days later they had taken the shape of a child's head or a woman's vagina. Or again: if anyone bit into a bean and crushed it in his teeth, then put the bean in the sun's rays, it would eventually smell like a murdered man.[43]

As with the connection between vegetarianism and transmigration, there is something more than primitive taboo at work here, for eating beans was considered dangerous to one's health. Because Pythagoras thought that too much sleep was unhealthy, long periods of wakefulness were the ideal. Eating meat and beans, he thought, encouraged drowsiness; hence, he discouraged them. If Pythagoras's denigration of beans is to be criticized, it should be on scientific grounds. In any event, his feelings about beans were so intense that some accounts suggest they caused his death when he was caught by the Kylonians. As the story goes, his flight was impeded because a field of beans was in his way and his own exhortation had always been not to tread on beans. I suppose if Richard III could lose a kingdom because of a horse, Pythagoras could lose one of many lives because of beans.[44]

(3) Most important for my purposes, the third foundation of

Pythagoras's vegetarianism was due to ethical considerations. He personally embodied what may be the cardinal insight of the Greeks: nothing in excess. He was never known to overeat, to be drunk, or to behave loosely. He tried to convince his followers not to eat meat, and to avoid other forms of overindulgence, e.g., picking up fallen crumbs, which were reserved for the heroes, as Aristophanes notes. He also tried to teach his followers how to be humane in preparing the foods they did eat.[45]

"Ethical considerations" does not refer only to Pythagoras's own moderation, but also to the care Pythagoras showed to the animals themselves. One should never destroy or damage any animal that is not harmful to mankind.[46] What right do we have to cause unnecessary suffering? And animals, besouled as they are, certainly are able to suffer.

As a matter of fact, the similarities between man and beast go even further. In the beginning (the golden age?), animals and humans used to speak the same language, as Plato also suggests in the *Statesman*. According to Iamblichus, the only major difference between animals and human beings for Pythagoras was that animals can only use internal speech, whereas humans have both internal and external speech.[47] (In chapter 6 we will explain this distinction more fully.)

The desire for superfluous nutriment may cause one to forget the sentience of animals. Therefore attention should be paid to the eating habits of youth from infancy (remember Aratus?). Youth should eat food conducive to a life of labor, endurance, *and* temperance. Once again, the claims regarding vegetarianism, bodily health, and strength are beyond the bounds of this book. It may be that Pythagoras bit off more than he could chew with his claims that vegetarianism is more healthy than meat-eating. Many in the contemporary debate are more cautious: the vegetarian need not show that his diet is healthier than a diet that depends on animals. He only needs to show that he can have *a* healthy diet without eating animals.

Pythagoras's vegetarianism is an expression of both the Delphic dictum "nothing in excess," and of another Greek commonplace: Apollo's exhortation to "know thyself" (gnothi seauton). Gorman expresses himself well concerning man's conscious-ness of his place in the Pythagorean universe:

> For Pythagoras man was intimately linked with the rest of the animal kingdom and did not enjoy any innate superi-ority over the other animals. Man was not the image of the divine, but a living being whose only distinguishing char-acteristic was his greater ability to be trained and partici-pate in intelligence. The real man was not his body, but the psyche. Of course, the other animals could be trained, as Pythagoras demonstrated in the case of the Daunian bear, and some men were capable of approaching the reality of the divine numbers by a rigorous programme of training and education, but man was still a member of the animal kingdom with none too many privileges; even his speech was not unique for Pythagoras contended that he could un-derstand the language of animals. The human is an animal which must shed this base origin by purification and train-ing in order to join the psychic forces which pervade the cosmos and which appear in all the various forms of life. . . . This involves a purification of the psyche which has an existence independent of the human animal so that the psychic self must become like the divine numbers or gods and not be yoked to a sick and dying animal. Resemblance to a god also allows the psyche to escape from reincarna-tion and all animal forms.[48]

Given this view of man's place in the universe, one can appre-ciate why Pythagoras would consider those who senselessly killed animals to be murderers.[49]

Quite apart from the doctrine of transmigration and the be-souled nature of animals, other reasons moved him to be a vege-tarian. That is, there is a distinctly modern character to his thought. Consider some evidence found in Porphyry's De absti-nentia: Pythagoras abstained from animal food and sacrifices (II, 28) not only because animals have the same soul as we do (III, 26), but also largely because he perceived animals as ra-

tional (*metechon tou logou*—III, 6). Thus, Pythagoras's abstinence may be due to his commiseration (*philoiktirmonos*—III,
20). In this context a Pythagorean banquet would be exhilarated
with a sense of justice by not eating meat; and for Porphyry, this
sort of banquet is superior to a Socratic banquet (presumably
like that in the *Symposium*) where hunger is the sauce of food
(III, 26).

Three more themes affect one's treatment of Pythagoras's vegetarianism: politics, environmentalism, and mathematics. Thus
far I have used the terms "Pythagoras" and "Pythagorean" inter-
changeably, but now some precision is needed. Not only is
there a history to vegetarianism among Pythagoras's followers,
but there is also an important difference in the way they ate
during his own lifetime.

There were two classes of Pythagoreans. Iamblichus not only
mentions them, but also gives us some indication of their re-
spective dietary habits.[50] One class of followers of Pythagoras
was called the *akousmatikoi*, who heard the teachings of the
master and followed them to a degree, but never penetrated the
inner mysteries of the cult and never had to enact stringent vegetarian ideals. The other class, the *mathematikoi*, were Pythagoreans in the strictest sense, hence the strictest vegetarians. At
their common meals, eaten in silence, they were prohibited
from eating superfluous and unjust food; the former included
wine, the latter anything animated. While eating they were encouraged to meditate on their previous days (even lives), making eating a part of life's general spiritual experience. That is,
food was the stuff out of which their prayers were made. Even
those who practice self-denial in eating can cherish food; perhaps they especially can cherish food. The *mathematikoi* were
not allowed to injure animals, but were most solicitously to
preserve justice toward them. Pythagoras practiced what he
preached to such an extent that he could instruct savage animals without punishing them. The *mathematikoi* also avoided
eating meat because it could defile the purity of *psyche* and prevent it from foretelling the future through dreams.

The *akousmatikoi* were not given free reign to eat whatever they wished, however. They could only eat some animal flesh, chiefly the hallowed meat of sacrificial victims. Occasionally Pythagoras ordered the *akousmatikoi* to observe periods of abstinence from all meat or from parts of it. A normal day in their lives is described by Iamblichus: They were often concerned with health of the body. They wrestled, jumped, engaged in pantomime. Their lunch consisted of bread and honey or the honeycomb, but they did not drink during the day. In the evening they walked and ate again. They made use of wine, bread, herbs, and the flesh of such animals as was lawful to immolate. They rarely fed on fish, nor on marrow, which was considered a messenger (*angelos*) from the gods; and they did not approve of hunters.

What does all of this have to do with politics? Two extremes can be posited, with the truth, I think, lying somewhere in between. This elect group of *mathematikoi* and their imitators must have been popularly regarded as a pack of religious fanatics, as far removed from politics as they were from sane eating. Gorman favors this interpretation: "It is certain that Pythagoras did not become involved in politics," as it was essentially a mystical, apolitical society he founded. The necessity of avoiding bloodshed was given such cosmic significance (often because of the unpleasant incarnations that might occur) that Pythagoras exhorted his followers to suffer an injustice rather than commit one.[51] In this sense Pythagoras was only political in the way Socrates (in the *Crito*) or Jesus (on the cross) were.

The other extreme would posit that Pythagoras was intensely political, and that his vegetarianism was part of a revolutionary ideology. Detienne outlines this view—although he does not hold to it—by tracing two tendencies that started in the fourth century, at least two centuries after Pythagoras's death.[52] Timaeus (not to be confused with the figure in Plato's dialogue) advocated the standard view of almost all commentators, including those I have primarily relied on: Porphyry, Iamblichus, and Diogenes Laertius.[53] This view states that Pythagoras was a vegetarian and encouraged his followers to do likewise. The other tendency is that of Aristoxenus, the originator of the view that

Pythagoras ate *all* types of meat, except from the ox and sheep.[54] We are left with two clear alternatives: either all of the other accounts are based on ignorance, or Aristoxenus (and his epigoni) is wrong. Insofar as the former seems unlikely, we should ask why Aristoxenus holds the position he does.

The Hellenistic era, of which Aristoxenus was a part, was skeptical of Pythagoras and increasingly rationalized his teachings. This reaction is akin to the agnosticism of our age. Aristoxenus, as a materialist and skeptic, did not want his picture of Pythagoras to include bizarre practices. But the real clue to Aristoxenus's account is the fact that remnants of the Pythagorean society survived at Tarentum until about the end of the fourth century, and it was on *this* society that Aristoxenus based many of his judgments about the original society at Croton. These Pythagoreans did eat meat, although there were always "true believers" who were vegetarian, and thus often received the brunt of comedic satire as late as the fourth and third centuries.[55]

Have I still evaded the political issue? Let me hit the nail right on the head. It seems fair to say that one of Pythagoras's aims in coming to Italy was to ameliorate the greed and luxury among the aristocracy, which created a shabby inequality among the citizens.[56] Iamblichus makes it quite clear that Pythagoras enjoined the politicians to abstain from eating animals; how could they persuade others to act justly if they themselves indulged in insatiable avidity by eating animals that are allied to us?[57] Somehow in his dealings with politicians and aristocrats (some of whom may have been *akousmatikoi*) Pythagoras came into contact with Milo, a noted glutton, a meeting which perhaps gave rise to Aristoxenus's belief that Pythagoras ate meat. (It should be remembered that Socrates was also associated with a less than desirable companion: Alcibiades.) Detienne is probably right when he holds that Pythagoras came to Italy to instill the virtues of moderation (*sophrosyne*), manliness (*andreia*), excellence (*arete*), and especially hard work (*ponos*).[58] Because Detienne views Pythagorean vegetarianism as a conscious attempt to reinstate the golden age, we may be blinded to the very practical aims of the sect.[59] One final note: Detienne convincingly shows the importance of smell in the preparation of food: aromas made their way to the gods; at the other end of the spectrum, beans—which symbolized Hades—lay in a bed of dung.[60]

In conclusion, Pythagoras's ideal was a political one in that his religiosity and philosophy were opposed to the status quo; he was no zealot, nor explicitly involved in party politics. The Pythagoreans (at least the *mathematikoi*) were always outsiders who lived in solitary places; even those in the cities found solace in the sacred groves and temples.[61] Haussleiter seems to account for the aberrant position of Aristoxenus by suggesting that some late Pythagoreans were corrupted by Cynic notions, reintroducing the concept of an easy transition from upward to downward transcendence (see chapter 2, above).[62]

Much more fruitful than the political approach to Pythagoras is the environmental one. Not only did Pythagoras show respect for gods, human beings, and animals, but also for trees, which should not be destroyed unless absolutely necessary.[63] Diogenes Laertius gives us Pythagorean distinctions, however, between plants and animals, which allow us to eat the former. All things that partake of heat (*thermos*) live; this is why plants live and presumably why we owe them *some* respect. But not all living things possess the sort of soul (*psyche*) man has, which is a detached part of aether: partly hot and partly cold. Note the tightrope Pythagoras is walking here. On the one hand, soul is closely connected with body, such that it is considered a part (albeit detached) of aether; on the other hand, what distinguishes soul from life is its immortality (*athanaton*) and its ungenerated "beginning." This makes the soul different from living bodies, which are both generated and mortal. Moving further up Pythagoras's scale of being, we find the soul of man, which is divided into three parts: intelligence (*nous*), passion (*thymos*), and reason (*phren*). Only *phren* is unique to man, i.e., animals are capable of *nous* and *thymos*.[64]

Because animals are capable of intelligence and passion, they are not to be eaten; because plants lack these, they can be eaten, yet must be respected to *some* degree.[65] Donald Hughes does the best job of trying to put in some intelligible order Pythagoras's attitudes toward the cosmos as a whole. His thesis holds that there are two conflicting tendencies in Pythagorean ethics. The first, the prescriptive content, does justice to the teachings of Pythagoras himself, which grew out of the Orphic nature mysticism and its prohibitions against taking life. These rules applied to certain plants as well as animals, in that the operative principle at work here is life, not a highly developed *psyche*.[66] Thus, the environment that fosters life was treated carefully. Pythagoras's followers were not supposed to muddy springs of water, nor be careless with their bodily wastes.

The other tendency Hughes notices is the idea of the separability of soul (*psyche*) from body (*soma*). The tricky word here is *zoon*, which sometimes means "animal" and at other times "a living thing." In this latter sense it can apply to plants. Although the Pythagoreans generally maintained that plants were ensouled (contra Diogenes Laertius's account, above), they were not the sort of *zoon* that possessed *nous* or *thymos* or *phren*. Long after Pythagoras's death the differences between plants and animals, and animals and human beings became exaggerated in Pythagorean circles. They therefore forfeited their status as a counterculture, to use Hughes's term.[67] The purification of the soul became equivalent to the denigration of the body, with the natural environment itself being the most encompassing of prisons. This led to an indifference or aversion to earthly bodies, including animal bodies. Vegetarianism remained, but for a different reason: not out of respect for *zoon*, *thymos*, or *nous*, but due to a fear of dangerous attachment to physical body. Rejection replaced affirmation.[68]

At the end of his article Hughes admits that his thesis depends on the distinction between *mathematikoi* and *akousmatikoi*. It was the latter that increasingly emphasized rejection of any concern with the natural environment (a severing which Hughes thinks is fatal to environmental ethics). The former continued a "pure" Pythagorean diet of milk, honey, and fruits, all of which "fall" naturally without destroying plant life, much less animal *psyche.* Some opponents to vegetarianism all of a sudden discover a sentiency in plants, thereby—they think—reducing the vegetarian's arguments to absurdity, for we will have nothing left to eat. They should consider the point that *even if* plants are sentient (see chapter 7) and should not be killed, there would still be plenty to eat.

This reintroduction of the *mathematikoi* leads me to mention, at long last, mathematics. Pythagoras's vegetarianism was connected with his mathematical speculation, in however tangential a way. Rather than offering animal sacrifices to the gods, the Pythagoreans offered their mathematical speculations.[69] These speculations, as is well known, emphasized the moral import of number, where moderation in all things was quantified. This applies to diet, as Porphyry tells us, in that Pythagoras always kept his body in the same balanced condition, as if on a scale.[70] Or more precisely, as Porphyry puts it, the Pythagoreans

> called "one" the reason for unity, and that for identity, and
> that for equality, and the cause of the *union and sympathy*
> of all things and of the preservation of that which remains
> the same. For truly the unity that exists between individu-
> als is of this sort, being united to the individuals and yet
> existing as a unit by reason of its participation in the first
> cause. Similarly they called "dyad" the dual reason for
> *diversity and inequality* and everything that is divided
> and in change and now one way, now another; for the na-
> ture of two is of this sort, even in individual objects (my
> emphasis).[71]

Interpreted rather loosely, it can be suggested that: (1) the "one" of the Pythagoreans refers, among other things, to the *union and sympathy* between man and animal, leading to vegetarianism; and (2) the "dyad" is a symbol of (or cause of?) the *difference* between man and beast, identified as *phren* by Diogenes Laertius, leading to man's Promethean status, which need not be exploited.

Although the one and the dyad are in tension, the continued presence of Pythagorean vegetarianism is one form or another indicates that the one prevailed, at least among the *mathematikoi* like Empedocles. This important thinker was a Pythagorean and a vegetarian. If my brief treatment of him here seems desultory, one should return to the remarks made about him in chapter 2. His conception runs as follows:

> There is no birth in mortal things, and no end in ruinous death. There is only mingling and interchange of parts, and it is this we call "nature." . . . When these elements are mingled into the shape of a man living under the bright sky, or into the shape of wild beasts or plants or birds, men call it birth; and when these things are separated into their parts men speak of hapless death.[72]

This cosmic harmony has Pythagorean roots, and was exhibited best, for Empedocles, in the golden age.[73] According to Aristotle, Empedocles even went so far as to suggest that plants are moved by desire, that they feel pleasure and pain, and have knowledge.[74] If Empedocles held this rather extreme view (extreme even for the *mathematikoi*), he may have benefited from a reconsideration of Pythagoras's dyad. In any event, Empedocles' vegetarianism was based not only on a belief in a return to the golden age, nor only on a somewhat confused conception of *zoon*, but also on the traditional grounds of transmigration. According to Diogenes Laertius, Empedocles himself was a bush, bird, and fish in previous lives.[75] He was also a woman, indicating that he had conquered sexism as well as speciesism through *metempsychosis*. Empedocles also had an aversion to beans.[76]

Empedocles is peculiar for two reasons: (1) his elevation of plants is unique; and (2) his justification of present vegetarian practices relies heavily on the myth of the golden age. Consider the following poem of his preserved by Porphyry:

> With painted animals and statues once
> Of sacred form, with unguents sweet of smell,
> The fume of frankincense and genuine myrrh,

> And with libations poured upon the ground
> Of yellow honey, Venus was propitious made.[77]

The similarities to Pythagoras are far more numerous, however. Both believed that animals participate in reason (*metechon tou logou*), and as Callicott notices, both gave moral status to non-human beings.[78] But more important—and here I am relying on Rodman—both had a deep sense of kinship with the nonhuman, especially animal life, a kinship which pushed them into a counterculture that was a motivating force for resisting the dominant, meat-eating culture.[79] These are the hallmarks of Pythagorean vegetarianism that will concern the remainder of this study: resistance to existing standards and the positing of a duty to animals.

4 SOCRATES THROUGH THEOPHRASTUS

THERE is little evidence that any of the philosophers before Socrates and after Empedocles were vegetarians. There is some indication that Heraclitus sustained himself on grass and herbs as he wandered in the mountains, but this was due more to his misanthropy than to vegetarian theory.[1] Nor was Socrates a vegetarian, an opinion shared by Porphyry and Haussleiter.[2] His attitudes toward eating, however, show some Pythagorean influences and prepare the way for a consideration of Plato and Aristotle, in that both were obviously admirers of Socrates.

What is most prominent about Socrates' view of eating is his indifference. It is said that when some rich men came to dinner his wife, Xanthippe, was ashamed of her meal. Socrates told her not to mind because if the visitors were reasonable they would put up with the meal, and if not there would be no need to care about them.[3] It is not that Socrates neglected his body, for he realized that no one could exist without nourishment, nor did he praise those who did neglect their bodies; rather, he disapproved of overeating.[4] Passages from the *Symposium* remind us that Socrates was once an able soldier (220A). Whenever he was invited for dinner he easily kept himself from overeating, and he advised those who could not do so to avoid food that stimulated appetite. We are reminded here of Pythagoras's choice of foods before going on a fast, treated above. And, according to Xenophon, Socrates jokingly alluded to Homer to make his point: Circe turned men into pigs by feeding them stimulating foods.[5]

This simplicity in eating harmed neither Socrates' health (he seemed quite fit when he took the hemlock at age seventy) nor his ability to enjoy the foods he did eat. Socrates also realized that his moderation was a privilege of the well-to-do, for the man who is hungry of necessity cannot afford to enjoy the little food he gets.[6] Socrates was, in fact, aware of issues concerning the just distribution of food.[7] In a chapter "On Table Manners," Xenophon describes how Socrates would equalize the portions at a "pot luck" dinner so none would be ashamed or hungry; for Socrates "to dine well" meant doing no harm to one's soul in the course of a meal, a Pythagorean commonplace.[8]

Socrates seems to have had some degree of sympathy for animals themselves. Animals are tempted by many of the same desires that tempt men: gluttony, lust, and so forth.[9] Although some animals—e.g., lions—are capable of exercising a considerable degree of courage (*Laches* 196E), and others (horses, dogs, etc.) are capable of voluntary, as opposed to instinctively involuntary, actions (*Lesser Hippias* 375A), these examples seem to be exceptions to the rule. As in the case of Renaissance humanism, Socrates' humanism, despite all of its commendable features, was hardly a boon to animals. According to Xenophon, Socrates believed that men were happier than beasts for several reasons: (1) speech is present in man, but lacking in animals, distinguishing Socrates from Pythagoras; (2) animals are limited to certain times when they can have sexual intercourse, whereas the occasions for sexual pleasure are readily available to humans throughout the year; and (3) perhaps most important, man has the solace of perceiving the existence of the gods.[10]

Socrates apparently concluded that in comparison to other living creatures, men were demigods. But he goes even further than this, according to Xenophon.[11] From the superiority of man, which even Pythagoras granted to a degree, Socrates seems to have concluded that animals are born and raised *for the sake of* man. To say the least, this transition needs support. To advocate, as Xenophon says Socrates did, that because men eat animals, animals *should* be eaten clearly begs the question. I will be looking to see if Plato or Aristotle can do a better job of defending the meat-eating position.

Before moving to Plato, however, Socrates' impact on some other Greeks should be noted. Simon of Athens, a friend of Socrates, wrote a dialogue "On Good Eating"; and Aristippus, another friend, concurred that excessive eating is unhealthy for the body, and is at least indirectly unhealthy for the soul.[12] More important, Socrates' antipathy toward overindulgence, concretely manifested at the end of the *Symposium* when only Socrates could walk away sober, influenced some fourth-century Cynics, who were often compared to Socrates.[13] Three of these Cynics deserve special attention (see also my discussion of the Cynics in chapter 2). (1) Diogenes was said to have jeered a man who paid court to kings, saying that the man could have avoided this indignity had he kept to a diet of vegetables. The reply to Diogenes was that if he did not wash vegetables he could have associated with men. Touché! Apparently Diogenes' (Socratic) antipathy toward gluttony led him to a vegetarian diet of vegetables, cheese, and figs.[14] But Diogenes lacked Socrates' subtle irony, and used the *blitzkrieg* approach. He once went up to a rather portly rhetorician and directly told him to let beggars have some of his paunch.[15] It is unclear, however, whether Diogenes really enjoyed criticizing others for their eating practices; it is also unclear whether he enjoyed eating in public, as he would have rather rubbed his belly to assuage hunger.[16]

(2) Another fourth-century Cynic, Crates, wrote a poem preserved by Diogenes Laertius, which rekindles the hope for a vegetarian utopia:

> There is a city Pera in the midst of wine-dark vapour,
> Fair, fruitful, passing squalid, owning nought,
> Into which sails nor fool nor parasite

Nor glutton, slave of sensual appetite,
But thyme it bears, garlic, and figs and loaves,
For which things' sake men fight not each with other,
Nor stand to arms for money or for fame.[17]

Once again, pacifism and vegetarianism are linked. Crates and his friend (3) Metrocles seem to have dined on lupins, an herb grown in manure (how fitting for a Cynic), whose seeds are edible.[18]

For Plato, as has been seen, the philosopher, ideally speaking, ought to be a vegetarian in order to (re)establish the link with animals found in the golden age. It is important to explore why this link was broken, a break which is symbolized by an ancient time of destruction when most animals perished (*Laws* 677E).

Given Plato's belief that an ideal rule (in the age of Cronus) would include concern for animals, it is curious that he seems to accept so easily the practice of meat-eating. He does not condemn hunting and butchering (*Statesman* 288E); nor does he object to raising livestock for consumption (*Laws* 847E). In fact, in the *Republic* (332C) the "culinary art" is described as the seasoning of meats (*opsois*), which are wholesome foods to eat (*Laws* 667B). Because they were considered wholesome, they were recommended to athletes (*Republic* 404C).

An apparent contradiction faces us. On the one hand, Plato views vegetarianism as an ideal worthy of striving for; on the other, he easily accepts less than ideal eating habits. Yet, this situation is not so much a contradiction as an example of the more general theory-*praxis* dilemma in Plato's philosophy. An illustration of this dilemma can be found in the *Republic* (501B): the philosopher must frequently "glance in two directions": he must keep his eye on the Forms of Justice, Beauty, and Sobriety, while at the same time he must look at the justice, beauty, or sobriety that he is trying to reproduce in "this" world. When he does this he must mingle and blend in with the cavelike world around him, all the while making sure that he does not completely lose sight of the light of the Forms. No easy task. When it comes to eating Plato seemingly abandoned his vegetarian ideal in order to concentrate on what he thought were more important problems regarding justice in "this" world. But he did not completely abandon the ideal.

In the *Gorgias* (464–65), Plato imposes restrictions on the art of cookery (*opsopoiike*). He does this through one of his favorite devices, the four-term analogy, of which he gives two examples:

sophistic: legislation :: rhetoric: justice

beautification: gymnastics :: cookery: medicine

The first analogy deals with health of soul, and suggests that legislation and justice are the true arts that deal with the soul: legislation gives one principles to live by, and justice offers a means of adjustment if legislation fails. Sophistic and rhetoric are types of flattery that imitate the true arts; anyone taken in by these forms of flattery can expect an unhealthy soul.

The second analogy considers bodily health: gymnastics gives precise guidelines for developing a healthy body, and medicine tells us how to cure the body if gymnastics fails (and eventually it must fail in that no science is perfect). Beautification (Grecian formula?) consists in devices that feign youth or health, but which cannot offer either. And cookery is a form of flattery that corresponds, in a way, to medicine. Cookery does not do the job of repairing the body as well as medicine, because it is a routine (*empeiria*) that tries to gratify and give pleasure (462D—presumably through sweetmeats, spicy sauces, and culinary exotica), whereas medicine more successfully uses (at times) unpleasant means to recover health. Cookery is not an art (*techne*) at all, because by exclusively devoting itself to pleasure without investigating the nature of pleasure, it fails to give a rational account (*logos*) of itself (500B, 501A). All of this makes it clear that Plato was very much interested in proper diet, for without such a concern, both bodily health and the health of the soul would deteriorate; thus, one who fell for mere cookery's bottle of "snake oil" could also easily fall for the rhetorical devices of the sophist. In Pythagorean fashion Plato wants diet (*dia-tetike*) to be brought within the control of a mathematically based medicine.[19]

Why did Plato not necessarily include abstinence from meat in such control? The aforementioned "two glances" passage in the *Republic* partially answers this question, but a more incisive look into Plato's thoughts on animals is needed. Animals, like men, can be anarchic (*Republic* 562E) because they are bursting with the spirit of liberty (*Republic* 563C). At times this unbridled energy can be channeled into courageous acts (*Laws* 963E). But more often this energy is irrational, an irrationality which is beastly (*theriodes*—*Republic* 571C) when found in the human animal (*Laws* 777B). Gaining wisdom comes when the beast within is tamed, analogous to the training of a real animal (*Republic* 493A). It is obvious that Plato regarded man as far superior to other animals, most notably because man, the rational animal, has the language and knowledge of the Forms (*Phaedrus* 249B).

Two sections from the *Timaeus* (69C–77C, 90E–92C) illustrate Plato's attitudes toward man and beast more precisely than the overworked (albeit beautiful) image of the charioteer in the *Phaedrus*. In the *Timaeus* Plato talks of three sorts of soul that man possesses: (1) Man has an immortal soul that is his spark of divinity. As in the case of the Christian man, made in his God's image, this spark of divinity allows Plato to retreat from his vegetarian ideal in order to eat animals. That is, man's superiority has been given a divine sanction. This soul is also the seat of reason and is located in the head. (2) Man has a mortal soul, which he shares with animals. It is not intrinsically irrational, in that part of it (in the upper chest, close to the head) is obedient to reason, and is the seat of passion, including pain. Because animals do experience pain for Plato, and yet can be eaten, Greek vegetarianism seems to hinge more than I have previously suggested on the question of whether animals have reason or divine sanction. The other part of the mortal soul is located in the lower belly, which acts as a receptacle for excess meat before excretion, so as to prevent gluttony. How convenient! (3) Finally, man has an unnamed, third kind of soul, which is his plantlike side and has no part of reason at all. This soul is located below the navel and completely lacks self-motion (i.e., freedom).

My consideration of Plato (and more important later on, of Aristotle) forces me to soften my criticism of the Christian attitude toward animals discussed in chapter 1. Christianity merely adopted and expanded some Greek themes: man's superiority due to a supposed divine sanction, man's superior reason. Yet there are some important differences in the Greek view, not the least of which is Plato's belief that the cosmos itself in its entirety is a living, breathing animal (see Timaeus 30C, 32D).

The appetitive part of the soul (epithymetikon) is the cause of the desire for food, which in the Phaedrus is symbolized by the wayward steed. It is this (the mortal and third souls of the Timaeus) which must be tamed.[20] But, as Rodman argues, the appetitive part of the soul often raises its ugly head, even in poetry.[21] Plato's indictment of the poets is partially due to his denunciation of mimesis, which is bestial in character; the poets allow a natural force like thunder or a growling animal to speak through them. Yet the eating of meat could be attacked on the same grounds: a mimesis of the carnivores. Perhaps one could object that eating meat is due more to a humanism than mimesis, as in the case of Socrates. But as Singer seems to suggest, Plato at this point would be in danger of succumbing to the Protagorean saying, "Man is the measure of all things," a dictum Plato would otherwise want to attack.[22]

Vegetarianism seems to have posed a continuing problem to Plato, which is understandable when one considers his similarities to Pythagoras: there is a tradition which suggests that Plato visited Egypt; and he apparently believed in metempsychosis.[23] Gorman notices that the Pythagorean idea of a communal mess hall (syssition) was kept alive by Plato.[24] But more subtle influences can also be found: Plato thought that aside from bread and relishes, no other foods were necessary (Repub-

lic 459A–C). He also believed, in Pythagorean fashion, that the origin of flesh is marrow, which God made out of triangles (*Timaeus* 73B).

It is not at all clear that Plato ever *completely* abandoned the Pythagorean vegetarian ideal, no matter how forceful were the mores of his meat-eating, cave-dwelling fellows. Three key texts force me to reserve the possibility that Plato was a vegetarian, or, at the very least, was supportive of vegetarian thought. The first is *Republic* 369D–373E, in which Socrates suggests— immediately after proposing the creation of the Republic—that the first and chief need of such a city is food: no small honor! Division of labor will produce not only food (barley meal, wheat flour, cakes), but enough food for a feast: relishes like salt, olives, cheese, onions, and greens; and desserts of figs, chickpeas, beans, myrtle berries, and acorns. These are foods of health and peace (presumably, peace with animals). Then Socrates is asked what foods would be eaten if he were founding not a Republic but a city of pigs. The reply: the delicacies (*tragemata*) now in use. These presumably include the sweetmeats (do pigs eat these?) that are noticeably absent from the diet of the citizens of Socrates' ideal city. That the Republic was to be a vegetarian city is one of the best-kept secrets in the history of philosophy.

The second text is from the *Laws* (781E–783B), and it shows that this problem spans the different periods of Plato's career. The Athenian makes it clear that the history of human institutions is immeasurably long, including the history of eating habits. Every sort of taste in meat and drink has at some time been exhibited, which leads one to wonder once again about the Greek practice of anthropophagy. Some people not only avoided such brutality, but also abstained from eating oxen meat and other more "acceptable" flesh. To eat such flesh was criminal, and to sacrifice it to the gods was a pollution; cakes and meal soaked in honey were considered much more pure. These unnamed people, who insisted on a universal vegetarianism like that of the Orphics, can be none other than the Pythagoreans. Now comes the key point: Clinias adds (with no objection from the Athenian, i.e., Plato) that this vegetarianism is a widely current and highly credible tradition (*kai sphodra legomena te ei-rekas kai pisteuesthai pithana*). As expounded in the *Republic*, food is the primary need of human beings, and vegetarianism is a current, highly credible way of meeting that need.

Finally, there is *Epinomis* 974D–975B. Here the Athenian (again, Plato) holds that some men who may have been considered wise long ago are no longer considered so. Vegetarians are not in this category. The legend of these men (again, the Pythagoreans?) has it that they put a check on the devouring of flesh, and absolutely condemned the consumption of some animals. Plato bestows on their rule a blessing of the first order: eating barley and wheat is still admirable, for although it may not in itself bring wisdom (not even Pythagoras believed this), such a diet does show an attempt to become the best person one can become. Although the mythical elements in Pythagorean vegetarianism are gone, the practice is still important to the life of one seeking understanding.

It is tragic that Plato left the impression that he totally abandoned vegetarianism and shunned its justification. As I have illustrated in these three passages (from the *Republic*, *Laws*, and *Epinomis*) and in chapter 2, there are not sufficient grounds for such an impression. Plato's desire to sustain vegetarian theory represents a plea to return to the richer Greek conception of man as a social being not intelligibly removable from his fellows or his natural environment—which includes besouled, sentient animals.[25] In the last analysis, Plato seems to tolerate meat-eating in the same way that Pythagoras tolerated the less rigorous practices of the *akousmatikoi*. In neither case does the thinker defend the practice of eating meat.

Before moving on to Aristotle, I will discuss some of the ways in which Plato affected his followers, in a manner similar to the legacy of Socrates. Menedemus, who personally knew Plato, would eat only olives as a symbolic gesture of rebuke for an extravagant host; he also became sick when he learned that he had inadvertently eaten meat, which perhaps shows a mixture of superstition and vegetarian ideals. Although it is not clear whether Menedemus was totally opposed to eating meat, it is

clear that doing so was rare for him. One of his pupils, Antigo-
nus, committed suicide through starvation, which was just as
much a violation of Greek moderation as overindulgence.[26]

Not all of Plato's followers in the Academy possessed the Pythagorean concern for animals. Speusippus, head of the Academy after Plato, is said to have thrown his dog into a well solely
for the sake of pleasure. But Xenocrates, a later head of the
school, was a protector of sparrows (remember Jesus' remark?);
and Polemo, who ushered the Academy into the third century,
even refused to punish a dog that bit him. Pyrrho, the skeptic, is
in many ways similar to Hume. He found the vanity of man
anathema, yet not so distasteful as to give up raising animals for
food, a practice that has some sort of vanity at its root.[27] Although he admired Homer for comparing men to lowly creatures like birds, there is no indication that he disapproved of
eating such animals.

Aristotle's position is as difficult to determine as Plato's. He
certainly permits meat-eating, at the very least, and there is
some evidence that he was opposed to vegetarianism. This is
regrettable in that, as Singer holds, it was Aristotle's view—
rather than the view of Pythagoras, or even Plato—that became
part of the dominant tradition regarding animals.[28] Of course,
no general treatment of Aristotle's thought on animals is to be
attempted here, which would be an extensive task given all Aristotle's biological works and the problems surrounding them.[29]
Rather, I will concentrate on a few short texts to determine why
he came to be regarded as a formidable opponent to philosophical vegetarianism.

The first selection is from *On the Soul*, in which Aristotle
discusses the power of thinking and psychic powers like the
nutritive, appetitive, sensory, and locomotive.[30] Plants have
only the nutritive power, whereas animals also have sensation
and appetite (which make possible the experience of pleasure
and pain), and some also have locomotion. Further, animals anticipate the future through desire, which is nothing but the appetite for pleasure. Only man, or an order similar or superior to

man, can think.[31] All of these distinctions make it clear that only the most general sort of definition can be given for soul (*psyche*), which is of little help when dealing with any particular species. Thus we must always ask: what *kind* of soul does a being have?

On the evidence of this passage one is tempted to say that if Aristotle were not a vegetarian, and apparently he was not, then he *should* have been. Several questions arise here. First, if animals experience not only pain but also the desire to avoid pain, why does the meat eater feel justified in causing them unnecessary pain? Rather than demanding that the vegetarian supply the proof that a being has rights (assuming that sentiency might be such a condition), as Margolis does,[32] perhaps the burden of proof should be on the meat eater to justify *his* position in light of the pain *he* causes. Second, should not the fact that Aristotle distinguishes between plants and animals give *some* sort of privileged status to animals not given to plants? And third, why does Aristotle deny animals the power of thinking (*dianoetikon*) and mind (*nous*)? No easy answer to this last question appears, but several possibilities come to mind. Perhaps Aristotle is merely attributing to man a type of knowledge through immediate intuition which animals lack; this interpretation receives some support from the text. Or again, perhaps he is attributing to man a type of intellectual freedom that animals lack. This position is supported by a passage in the *Eudemian Ethics* (1222B19–21), where man is set apart from all other animals because of his reason, which can function as a director (*arche*) for his actions.

More specifically, animals are different from inanimate natural bodies because, although both require external forces to explain their movements, animals require external forces perceived as having significance *for them*. Animals are self-movers not because they avoid being moved by objects of desire, but because when they move, the cause of motion is seen as such by their souls, without appeal to *nous*.[33] Aristotle also seems to deny *nous* to animals because he denies they have beliefs; this involves the debated issue of whether they are capable of conceptual awareness, an issue that also concerned Plato (*Theaetetus* 186B–C).

For whatever reason, it seems that Aristotle *does* deny the power of thinking to animals. Porphyry, however, claims (without specific references) that Aristotle did allow animals to participate in reason (*logou*), and those animals whose powers were more developed were regarded as prudent (*phronimotera*). If ferocious animals appear to lack reason, it is probably due to a lack of food.[34] Inasmuch as we have Aristotle's texts to consider, I will let him speak for himself and deal later with Porphyry's interpretation.

What makes Aristotle's opposition to vegetarianism likely, but by no means certain, is a passage in the *Politics* (Bk. I, chaps. 5 and 8). Aristotle makes it clear that the rule of the mind over the passionate element is natural in man, and the equality of the two or the rule of the inferior is harmful. The same holds true of the relationships between man (i.e., mind) and animals (merely appetitive souls). Some tame animals do come closer to human nature than others which are wild, but even tame animals need the rule of man in order to survive.

For the sake of argument I will grant Aristotle his hierarchy of mind and passion, but problems nonetheless appear: (1) Why does this hierarchy necessarily follow in the relationships between man and animal? (2) Why does Aristotle deny reason to the higher, tame animals? (3) How does he know that certain animals could not survive without us? Even though Aristotle might not have been aware of species that could not survive *with* us (i.e., those we have made extinct), he should have supplied more evidence for his dependency thesis.

These unsupported theses are thrown into sharp relief when Aristotle applies the same principles to human relations. The male is by nature superior to the female; one rules and the other is ruled. The modern reader might find it even more incredible to read that this principle of natural rule and superiority extends to *all* mankind:

When there is such a difference as that between soul and body, or between men and animals (as in the case of those whose business is to use their body, and who can do nothing better), the lower sort are by nature slaves, and it is better for them as for all inferiors that they should be under the rule of a master. . . . Whereas the lower animals cannot even apprehend a principle; they obey their instincts. And indeed the use made of slaves and of tame animals is not very different.

After having considered the gentle Pythagorean ethic it would take a great amount of apologetics (e.g., rationalizing that slavery was a traditional part of Greek culture) on the part of Aristotle's defenders to make him tolerable here. At least five points should be made: (1) He obviously has not proven that males are by nature superior to females. (2) Nor *a fortiori* has he shown that his principle of superiority can apply to all mankind. (3) It is not clear how Aristotle can know why slaves have a natural predisposition to use their bodies—nor does he know that they can do nothing better (see, for example, the slave boy in Plato's *Meno*). (4) No evidence is cited to show why slaves are better off as slaves. (5) No argument is provided to show that animals are totally governed by instinct; recent work suggests otherwise, including the famous experiments in teaching sign language to apes.[35] It may be that animals have undeveloped potential like the slave boy of Meno.

This passage in the history of philosophy perhaps most clearly establishes the link among sexism-racism-speciesism. Why is it so obvious to us that the principle of natural superiority is a morally dangerous notion when applied to sex and other types of discrimination? And why exclude sentient, nonhuman animals (sentient even on Aristotle's theory) from consideration as beings worthy of respect? If Aristotle claims natural superiority, is not the burden of proof on *him* to prove his case regarding animals? These are the kinds of questions Aristotle's defenders would have to respond to. Aristotle himself must have thought that human superiority over animals was too obvious to require argument, and the fact that he thought the same about women and slaves must nag at most modern readers.[36] If he were wrong in these two instances. . . . As Salt noticed, oppression and cruelty are invariably founded on a lack of imaginative sympathy, or on a failure to avoid the fallacy of special pleading.[37]

When Aristotle's defense of the slavery of animals is tied to his belief that at least light meats (bird meats?) are digestible and healthy (*Nichomachean Ethics* 1141B14–23), one has the outline of a defense of meat-eating. Although Wieland forces the critic of Aristotle to be more precise, criticisms seem to hold nonetheless.[38] For Wieland, the above passage should not be interpreted as implying a universal teleology where animals are ordered in and of themselves for the sake of man. Rather, Aristotle is concerned with the practical question of how man is to establish himself in the world and make use of its bounty. What Wieland fails to answer are these questions: (1) How can Aristotle legitimately "content himself with popular notions for the purpose he has in mind" regarding animals? And (2), can man legitimately "put *all* other things at his service and *use* them" even if these "things" (animals?) do not have an innate tendency to serve man? (my emphasis).

At least Aristotle is consistent in assigning certain prerogatives to animals over plants; the latter exist for the sake of the former (again, see *Politics*, Bk. I, chap. 8). And for Aristotle, if nature makes nothing in vain, the inference *might* still be (contra Wieland) that she has made all animals for man's sake; thus, the art of hunting is a naturally just war. But even if the principle of natural superiority is true, it does not follow that animals exist for the sake of man. It is not clear why a teleological approach to nature necessitates the enslavement of animals.

Regarding animals, Aristotle is no Descartes, however.[39] That is, animals for Aristotle were not just unfeeling machines, but living, breathing, sentient creatures. Thus, to label Aristotle a speciesist is perhaps a little misleading, as Rodman argues:

The more subtle objection to Aristotle applies to him insofar as he followed the moral philosophy of Socrates and Plato and assumed as axiomatic the proposition that every species ought to act as to maximize its differentiae rather than its genus. The premise of man's world-alienation (and of his self-alienation—the tyranny of rationality over the rest of the psychic ecosystem) is engraved in this basic axiom of classical moral philosophy, but little attention is paid to it, partly because it is so basic, partly because it is still so widely shared, not only by modern philosophers but also by the colloquial projections of ordinary language, which still oppose the truly human to bestial cruelty and to merely vegetative existence.[40]

As a critic of Aristotle, Rodman has done well. But my treatment of Plato and, of course, of Pythagoras should cast doubt on the claim that the tyranny of human rationality was a basic axiom of all classical moral philosophy.

What causes the difference between Plato and Aristotle? These two giants of ancient philosophy both accept what Matthews calls the "principle of psychological continuity": acts, states, and functions in lower animals mimic those in higher animals.[41] But their reasons for this principle are quite different. As Matthews states the case for Plato (relying on *Phaedo* 81D–82B and *Timaeus* 90E–91C):

Plato accepted the Pythagorean idea of metempsychosis, or transmigration of psyches. In principle it is possible, he thought, that your psyche or mine might next animate a dog or a fish. Psychological acts, states and functions in lower animals model those in higher animals for the very good reason that the souls or psyches of lower animals are the functional equivalent of degenerate human psyches. In fact Plato sometimes suggests that your soul in its next incarnation may go to some human or sub-human animal whose characteristic virtues, that is, whose functional excellences, are most like those you develop in this life.

Matthews contrasts Aristotle, using *On the Soul* (Bk. II, chap. 3):

> Aristotle accepted the Principle of Psychological Continu-
> ity on quite a different basis. His threefold classification of
> psyches—(1) plant or nutritive souls, (2) animal or sensi-
> tive souls and (3) human or rational souls—already incor-
> porates limited continuity, since Aristotle supposed that
> the psychic functions of sensitive souls include nutritive
> functions and the psychic functions of human souls in-
> clude both sensitive and nutritive functions. But the Aris-
> totelian classification scheme also suggests radical discon-
> tinuity. It suggests that there is nothing in plants similar or
> analogous to reason in human beings. Aristotle counters
> this suggestion of discontinuity in various places, but no-
> where more eloquently than in . . . the beginning of Book
> VIII of the *History of Animals*.

In this passage from the *History of Animals* Aristotle is willing
to say that

> just as in man we find knowledge, wisdom, and sagacity, so
> in certain animals there exists some other natural poten-
> tiality akin to these . . . so that one is quite justified in say-
> ing that, as regards man and animals, certain psychical
> qualities are identical with one another, whilst others re-
> semble, and others are analogous to, each other.[42]

Perhaps this passage led to Porphyry's generous treatment of
Aristotle, alluded to above.

There were good reasons for both Plato and Aristotle to be
vegetarians. Plato seems to have realized this, but reluctantly
surrendered, at times, to a more popular principle of psychological discontinuity, apparently held by his mentor, Socrates.
It is less clear that Aristotle realized the consequences of his
theories regarding animals, but in fairness to him we should
read what he has to say in *On the Parts of Animals* (Bk. I,
chap. 5):

For in all natural things there is something wonderful. And just as Heraclitus is said to have spoken to the visitors, who were wanting to meet him but stopped as they were approaching when they saw him warming himself at the oven —he kept telling them to come in and not worry, "for there are gods here too"—so we should approach the inquiry about each animal without aversion, knowing that in all of them there is something natural and beautiful.

The vegetarian would no doubt think that Aristotle was on the right track here, and wonder what caused him to veer away from it. More likely than a genetic explanation for his apparent later movement away from Plato is the fact that his awe at animal varieties is due to a clinical-scientific spirit which "objectifies" all of nature. This attitude is obviously alive and well in the contemporary world, and constitutes one of the greatest obstacles to a fair hearing for vegetarian claims.

Other passages from Aristotle exhibit this same ambivalence toward animals. In the *Nichomachean Ethics* (Bk. VI, chap. 7), he narrows the gap between human beings and animals by admitting, on the one hand, that even human beings are lowly when compared with other beings in the universe and, on the other, that some animals even have a type of low-level practical wisdom which comes from foresight. But in *De Motu Animalium* (701B1–15), animals are paradoxically compared to *automata*, which Nussbaum translates as "puppets," thereby avoiding association with Cartesian "machines."[43] Even if animals are incapable of happiness (*eudaemonia*) because they are incapable of contemplation—as we learn in the *Nichomachean Ethics* (Bk. X, chap. 8)—one would nonetheless expect from Aristotle *at least* some indication that the sentiency of animals places restraints on our enslavement of them.[44] Theophrastus accomplishes what his teacher did not: he sifted through Aristotle's complicated theories on animals to deduce vegetarianism as a conclusion.

"Aristotle's student Theophrastus has long stood in the

shadow of his teacher, and has thus been underestimated."[45] This remark by Hughes is nowhere more true than in his awareness of the (vegetarian) implications of the principle of psychological continuity. This principle did not force Theophrastus to deny a purpose in nature. But the *telos* of things in nature is not always evident, nor is the practical *telos* of "things" available for our use, as Aristotle may have assumed when he said that plants and animals exist for the sake of mankind. As Hughes has it:

> Theophrastus' willingness to regard the natural environment as fulfilling its own purposes, interrelating with man but at the same time autonomous, yielded in the history of ancient and medieval thought to the anthropocentric teleology of his teacher, Aristotle.

We learn from Diogenes Laertius that Theophrastus wrote several works on animals.[46] But perhaps his status as the "father of ecology"[47] and his practice of vegetarianism were the result of his studies of plants, the most extensive in antiquity.[48] More than any Greek philosopher, he understood the differences between plants and animals, not the least of which was the inability of the former to experience pain.[49]

Haussleiter has pointed us in the right direction if we are to discover exactly why Theophrastus was a vegetarian.[50] The right direction is Porphyry. In *De abstinentia* we can see that Theophrastus's vegetarianism was intimately connected with a desire to return to primeval perfection (see chapter 2). Ancient libations were performed with sobriety when water was offered, and later, when offerings were honey, oil, and wine (II, 20). When animal sacrifices were finally initiated, not only did meat-eating come into vogue but also atheism cropped up as a reaction against the anger of the gods when animals were deliberately killed (II, 7; also II, 32).

Vegetarianism, however, is not just a religious matter for Theophrastus; it is also a matter of ethics, for to unnecessarily kill animals is unjust (II, 11–12). He holds that pestilence and war that damaged crops provided the occasion for the first eating of animals, but now that vegetal food is abundant there is no need to sacrifice or eat animals. Besides, the gods consider the fruits of the earth to be the most beautiful and honorable gifts. Piety and justice require that we prevent injuring others when we can. And animals *can* be injured, as opposed to plants, as Haussleiter notices, for they are capable of passion (*pathe*), perception (*aistheseon*), and reason (*logismoi*).[51] Theophrastus, as has been stated, does not see animals as existing only for the sake of man. But even if they were created for the sake of man, it does not follow that we can injure them or take their lives (II, 12). Theophrastus seems to suggest that there is a difference between existing for the sake of something else (i.e., an aid to) and looking to something else for the very permission to exist. Besouled animals, and not plants, are too honorable (*timioteron*) for this state of affairs to be tolerated.

Perhaps in deference to his teacher, Theophrastus does not wholly condemn the meat eater, but then again he does not make concessions to him, as Plato did. Rather, he gradually tries to move the meat eater "back to" the vegetarian position. If one believes that the gods demand animal sacrifice, then sacrifice animals, but do not eat their flesh. That is, Theophrastus is aware of how taste can often be rationalized in the form of religious duty. The Jews are favorably cited in this regard for burning their victims whole without eating the flesh (II, 26), which may or may not be an accurate rendering of the Old Testament practice. Or from another direction, in ancient times when human beings had to be sacrificed to the gods (Iphiginia?), men never interpreted this to mean that the victims were to be eaten (II, 53). Why so in the case of animals (III, 25), especially when *all* animals are allied through passion (*pathon*) and some capacity for intellection (*phronousi*)?

Like Plato, Theophrastus saw worth in the Spartan practice of common meals, which encouraged frugality in eating (IV, 4), even if they did not prevent meat-eating. Yet in the end Theophrastus (along with Dicaerchus; see chapter 2) must be considered an Aristotelian who partially abandoned his teacher's attitude toward animals, largely because he attended more carefully to some of the master's ideas than did the master himself. The soul of man is not just an inhabitant of the body, but an animating principle that gives itself wholly to the body (IV, 20), painfully experiencing every blow to the flesh. No less is true of nonhuman animals.

5 THE HELLENISTIC ERA, THE ROMANS, AND PLUTARCH

PASSMORE contends that the Stoics thought it obvious that animals were devoid of reason, that providence cared nothing for animals, and that they lacked rights. His view is reinforced by Pohlenz: "Against the Pythagoreans the Stoics vigorously defended the view that there is no legal or moral tie of any kind between man and animal." Passmore is amiss in his claim that even the most unorthodox Stoics stood firm in their denigration of animals during the 500-year history of the Stoic school. In general, however, the Passmore-Pohlenz position is on the mark. Chrysippus, one of the most important Stoics, even flirted with a view that was dangerously close to Cartesianism: animals do not really feel, but only "as it were" feel. And in Humean fashion the skeptical Sextus Empiricus argued against the presumption of (Stoic) men who set themselves above nature as absolute rulers, or who suppose that animals completely lack rationality.[1]

Following Aristotle, the Stoics (including Cicero) defined animals in terms of an extrinsic teleology, where plants existed for animals and animals existed for men.[2] Animals cannot be members of our community of concern primarily because they lack reason—i.e., human beings could not possibly be just to animals because justice is possible only between those who *share* values.[3] It is paradoxical to note (contra Pohlenz) that beasts and men shared a common law in Greek thought, particularly with respect to the treatment of human *and* animal parents and children, a fact the Stoics must have recognized.[4] Perhaps the Stoics arrived at their position because of the popularity of social contract theory from Protagoras on; but not even human beings have ever contracted to be moral or social. By admitting that the social contract is only a thought experiment or implicit agreement, rather than a historical fact, doubt would be cast on the Stoic belief that a primitive contract places duties on us. Further, as Clark so forcefully states:

> Rationalistic attempts to find an absolute stability in the moral domain, now that God is reckoned dead, are at once implausible in themselves and ineffective to produce any absolute dichotomy between man and beast. They are really no more than desperate and often unintelligible reconstructions of the Stoic ethic.

Or what is perhaps more likely is the Stoic belief that the irrational is totally beneath consideration. Like Chrysippus, we are inclined to believe that animals are so much protoplasmic stuff without individual personalities; all cows are grey in the dark of our own blindness.[5]

Much of what we know of Stoic objections to vegetarianism comes from Porphyry.[6] The principal objection seems to be that justice would be confounded if extended to irrational (animal) nature. Analogously, human beings do not associate with or acknowledge the laws of some foreign polity, for to do so is dishonorable. In addition, we could not live without eating animals; and even if we could survive on plants, we would be reduced to a brute level of living if we reject what animals are capable of affording. This Stoic position echoes Genesis through an allusion to Zeus's gifts, described by Hesiod:

> To fishes, savage beasts, and birds, devoid
> Of justice, Jove to devour each other
> Granted; but justice to mankind he gave.[7]

Therefore, in that animals are incapable of receiving justice, we are not duty-bound to give it. Finally, he who cuts the throat of a sheep or ox does no more injury than he who cuts down a tree, especially if the doctrine of transmigration is brought into play.

My reactions to these Stoic views are several: (1) It is by no means clear why animals *must* be regarded as irrational; Plutarch will show us the intelligibility of perceiving them as rational. (2) Regardless of whether animals are irrational or nonrational, it is by no means clear why rationality is the sole criterion, or even a necessary condition, for justice (e.g., all would acknowledge, I think, that a retarded person could be treated unjustly). (3) It is difficult to understand how distributing justice to animals would necessarily confound human justice, unless justice were some sort of finite pie, some of whose slices were being nibbled on by animals. But justice is hardly this sort of thing. (4) To consider it a dishonor to associate with a foreign polity is certainly provincial; the same could be said of those who analogously think that associating in a friendly way with animals is a dishonor. (5) It *is* possible for us to live without eating animals. The repeated attempts to suggest otherwise (St. Thomas, Kant, et al., to the present day) indicate how the meat eater is often blind to the healthiness of a vegetarian diet. (6) It does not follow that we will be reduced to the level of brutes if we do not use animals in ways afforded us (e.g., for food). Eating another being is not a necessary condition for establishing a difference from it. (7) As suggested above, to hold that we have a duty to be just to animals (either because of their sentience or rationality)—even though they are not capable of being just in return—is not odd, for we acknowledge duties of justice to many other beings who cannot reciprocate, e.g., infants, the mentally enfeebled, the senile. (8) Finally, and perhaps most important, the Stoic attempted *reductio ad absur-dum*—which suggests that if we show justice to animals we will have to do so as well to plants, thereby threatening our own existence as just beings—fails in that there are notable differences between plants and animals, at least in degree of sentiency if not in kind. Clark is correct in saying that there is a certain hypocrisy in this Stoic argument, i.e., the Stoic is remarkably sympathetic to oak trees when his torments of sheep and oxen are brought to his attention.[8]

Porphyry's reaction to the Stoic view of animals shows an awareness not only of the argument from sentiency, but also, surprisingly, of the argument from marginal cases:

> To compare plants, however, with animals, is doing violence to the order of things. For the latter are naturally sensitive (*aisthanesthai*), and adapted to feel pain, to be terrified and hurt (*kai algein kai phobeisthai kai blaptesthai*); on which account also they may be injured (*adikeisthai*). But the former are entirely destitute of sensation, and in consequence of this, nothing foreign, or evil (*kakon*), or hurtful (*blabe*), or injurious (*adikia*), can befall them. For sensation is the principle of all alliance (*Kai gar oikeioseos pases kai allotrioseos arche to aisthanesthai*). . . . And is it not absurd (*alogon*), since we see that many of our own species (*anthropon*) live from sense alone (*aisthesei monon*), but do not possess intellect (*noun*) and reason (*logon*) . . . that no justice is shown from us to the ox that ploughs, the dog that is fed with us, and the animals that nourish us with their milk, and adorn our bodies with their wool? Is not such an opinion most irrational and absurd?

Porphyry is crystal clear as to which Stoics he has in mind.[9] Zeno and his followers assert that the principle of alliance or intimacy (*oikeioseos*) should be used to determine which beings deserve justice, but for Porphyry this begs the question. What he needs is some criterion for alliance, some way to determine how we will group nature into the various households of edible and inedible beings. For all those beings who think that unnecessary suffering ought to be avoided—i.e., for *at least* all rational human beings—sensation (*aisthanesthai*) is a principle of alliance that must be considered. Using this criterion, Porphyry's comparison of plants and animals is instructive. If we suggest that sentiency is an insufficient standard for being justly treated, we eliminate many of our own species who live by sense alone, without reason (*alogon*). And if we "lower" our standards to include all human beings, we must be willing to include animals capable of sensation, among which would be cows, pigs, and chickens. At this point a defender of the Stoics would either have to admit his inconsistency or abandon his opposition to infanticide, mercy killings of the retarded, and so on. Hardly a nice position to find oneself in! Porphyry has given a remarkably modern argument from marginal cases against opponents of vegetarianism; a pity that those who use similar arguments today show no awareness of the sophistication of ancient vegetarianism.[10]

Furthermore, Porphyry argues against Zeno by suggesting what is perhaps too obvious for us to take seriously: animals do give us something in return for our justice. Dogs offer companionship, cows and goats give milk, sheep produce wool, and the like. Porphyry also attacks Chrysippus for his claim that the gods made animals for man's sake, and that whatever soul animals possess was given by the gods so that animals would taste better. "The best of all possible worlds," Chrysippus might say as an ancient Pangloss. Carneades, a skeptical critic of Chrysippus, nonetheless maintained a Stoic attitude toward animals by suggesting that everything produced by nature is benefited (*opheleitai*) when it obtains its end. This is fine as far as it goes, but by "benefit" Chrysippus and Carneades mean only what is useful (*euchrestian*) to man. Such anthropocentrism, Porphyry seems to say, is inconsistent both with Stoic concern for cosmic *logos* and with the less ambitious philosophical anthropology of the skeptics.

Regarding Passmore's remark that *all* Stoics held this view of animals, even Porphyry admits that some unnamed Stoics had accurately written about these topics.[11] And Diogenes Laertius

attests to the simplicity of Zeno's own life—in that the founder
of Stoicism usually only ate loaves and honey.[12] He quotes Philemon on Zeno, saying:

> This man adopts a new philosophy.
> He teaches to go hungry: yet he gets
> Disciples. One sole loaf of bread his food;
> His best dessert dried figs; water his drink.

Haussleiter tries to make sense of this side of the Stoics by stat-
ing that despite their extrinsic teleology regarding animals,
many Stoics ate like vegetarians because of the benefits of asceticism.[13] He applies this thought especially to Posidonius of
Apameia (second century B.C.), but also to Musonius and two of
his followers in the first century A.D.: Dion and Epictetus.[14] The
distinctive character of Musonius's teaching was his insistence
on the close connection between theory and practice; knowledge not applied to improving man's ethics was useless.[15]

Also in the first century A.D., is the peculiar case of the Roman Seneca. He normally spouts standard Stoic doctrine in his
essays and letters. But in a letter "On Instinct in Animals," although he does not indicate a vegetarian diet, he does criticize
the anthropocentric heart of Stoicism.[16] He agrees that nature
has set man above other animals (3), but this does not necessarily mean that animals lack feeling about their own constitution (5). Nor does Seneca believe that all animal actions are
compelled (non voluntas). The alertness of animals indicates
that they move of their own accord; even when pain checks
their struggle they persevere in the attempt to reach the object
of their wishes. The turtle that is turned on its back will twist
and grope until it is upright; this is no different from the child
who tries to walk, even when his repeated falls bring tears to
his eyes (8–9). Although animals may not be able to define the
term "soul"—or "justice" or "social contract"—this does not
mean that they lack consciousness of their constitution (11).
Many college students cannot define these terms, yet our duties
toward them are not diminished. Seneca ends his defense of
animals by arguing that although we do not know how animals

understand death, it is clear that they have an understanding (*intellectum*) of it. Like his Pythagorean teacher, Sotion, Seneca was more concerned with the practical conclusion to forswear flesh than with the precise argument that led to it.[17] Although, according to Gorman, Seneca kept alive the Stoic denigration of animals by maintaining silence about the barbarous treatment of animals in the amphitheater, he was decidedly (and uncharacteristically) non-Stoic in what he did say about animals.[18]

The problems surrounding Seneca's vegetarianism are connected with the central problem with his thought. He probably had the ability to become a more original thinker, but his up-and-down career in the courts of Caligula and Nero no doubt affected what he could say and do. In Epistle CVIII he clearly agrees with his teachers Sotion and Sextius in their reasons for supporting vegetarianism, which were grand ones (*magnifica*): in that sufficient nourishment is possible without shedding blood, killing animals is cruel. Seneca tells us that he became a vegetarian, and after a year or so found the practice not only moral but also delightful. Yet he was induced to abandon vegetarianism because it became the object of imperial suspicion. Williams holds, however, that Seneca must have continued practicing vegetarianism in private life, causing some sort of intellectual schizophrenia.[19] Rather than criticize the emperor, Seneca surprisingly blames (Stoic?) teachers for the general unpopularity of vegetarianism. They teach one how to dispute rather than how to live; they love words more than wisdom. (Note the analogy between Seneca's unnamed teachers and some rather commonplace criticisms of contemporary analytic philosophy.) In Epistle XCV, Seneca tries to isolate the psychological cause of meat-eating: for emperors and teachers alike it is covetousness (*ambitio*). Whether this same cause prevented Seneca from publicly maintaining a vegetarian diet is difficult to determine.

Haussleiter correctly judges that Epicurus was like some of the Stoics: his diet was apparently meat-free. But to call him a vegetarian would demand some qualification, in that he was only interested in mankind, not in animals.[20] It seems that Epicurus lived in a garden where friends would live with him in a communal simplicity that considered bread and water sufficient food. A bit of cheese made a feast.[21] Although this simplicity may have benefited Epicurus, it did little for the animals, who find themselves outside the bounds of justice for two reasons: (1) They are not able to make covenants. My criticisms of this Stoic commonplace would apply *a fortiori* to Epicurus. And (2), animals are not even capable of being harmed (*mede blaptesthai*).[22] This is probably a consequence of the previous reason, and not a denial of animal sentiency altogether. Also, Epicurus's criticism of superstitious religious beliefs may be connected with his eating practices. His garden (*kepos*) provided self-sufficiency, made possible by a simple life dependent on vegetal food.[23]

Epicurus's main insight regarding food seems to be that one should avoid those foods which, when enjoyed, eventually lead to an unacceptable feeling of privation.[24] This would rule out meat-eating even for those who had nagging doubts about the possibility that meat-eating was wrong. With Epicurus's weak anthropocentric foundation, however, the vegetarian position could not last too long among the Epicureans. Epicurus's admirer, Lucretius, was not opposed to meat-eating. This is understandable in light of Epicurus's famous contention that an individual's (even an animal's) death could not be a misfortune, because when he is alive he cannot suffer it and when he is dead he cannot suffer anything. But as Sapontzis points out, the living *can* suffer the misfortune of death—even if killed "painlessly"—if by their death they lose the possibility of further happiness. That is, the right to life is a part of the right not to suffer unnecessarily, inasmuch as life is essential to *avoid* suffering. Epicurus's simplicity nonetheless rubbed off on two of his followers—Polystratus and Philodemus—who kept his bastardized vegetarianism alive for a while. But one of the foremost opponents to vegetarianism is Epicurus's disciple, Hermarchus.[25]

Hermarchus's arguments include the following: The rational consideration of utility would prevent one from slaughtering another human being, but because few are capable of this restraint, law is needed to keep the vulgar in awe. The first lawgivers, however, did not forbid us to kill other animals, inasmuch as men could not survive if they did not defend themselves against animal attacks. Thus, the slaughter of animals and the abstinence from slaughtering men have a common end: the safety of the individual and society. When the wild beasts were expelled, the slaughter of animals was given a new justification: it provided nutriment just as it had previously supplied safety. Destroying everything noxious, and preserving that which is subservient to its extermination, contribute to a fearless life.

With Porphyry's help it should not be hard to dismantle this position: (1) The premise that it is only fear that compels human beings to refrain from behaving with impunity is questionable. The Epicurean version of a social contract is just as weak, if not weaker, as the position Glaucon defends in Book Two of the *Republic*. (2) Even if this position is defensible, now that wild animals no longer threaten us there would seem to be no justification, on Epicurean grounds, to kill animals. The fact that they provide nutriment begs the question, for even the flesh of human beings can do this. (3) The Epicureans, along with many of the Stoics, actually *help* the vegetarian position by providing many examples of healthy lives led without animal nutriment. Porphyry supports Haussleiter's contention that most Epicureans who were contemporaries of Epicurus satisfied themselves with vegetables and fruits. These adherents filled their writings with remarks on how little nature requires, and that its necessities may be sufficiently remedied by slender and easily procured food. To legitimately kill animals, by their account, one's defense would entirely rest on the "dictates" of taste.[26]

Discussing the Romans at this point is expeditious, in that their attitudes toward animals were built upon Greek foundations. Brumbaugh synthesizes into four categories the Greek views of animals that informed the Romans:[27] (1) *Animism*—the view that animals and persons have indestructible souls that change the bodies they animate. The Orphics and Pythagoreans are prime examples of this view. (2) *Mechanism*—the idea that men and animals are mere machines, e.g., as described by the atomists.[28] Although this view seems to be the exact opposite of animism, both share the belief that human beings and animals are alike. (3) *Vitalism*—a view that only sees a continuity, not an identity, between the vital principles of animals and men. This view, found mainly in Aristotle, was influenced by the Greek medical tradition, and emphasized the interdependence of soul and body. (4) *Teleological anthropocentrism*—a view that suggests that everything in the world was created for human pleasure, offering a "common sense" attitude (reborn through capitalist self-interest) that appealed to Xenophon.[29]

I see some problems with Brumbaugh's synthesis. For example, the suggestion that the Epicureans were mechanists ignores the teleological anthropocentrism of their views; although the neoplatonists tended to be animists, they also emphasized the interdependence of soul and body, and so on. But Brumbaugh is certainly correct in holding that although all four tendencies could be found in Roman thought, teleological anthropocentrism definitely won the day. All are (or should be) familiar with the cruelty of the Romans toward animals. And as Brumbaugh points out, unless one recognizes some similarity between man and animal, there is no pity, fear, or sense of victory in killing such animals for entertainment.

The purpose of the "games," as Singer holds, was not just entertainment; they also served to toughen an empire built and maintained through wars of conquest.[30] The nineteenth-century historian Lecky gives a moving account of the Roman games:

> The simple combat became at last insipid, and every variety of atrocity was devised to stimulate the flagging interest. At one time a bear and a bull, chained together, rolled in fierce combat across the sand; at another, criminals dressed in the skins of wild beasts were thrown to bulls, which were maddened by red-hot irons, or by darts tipped with burning pitch. Four hundred bears were killed on a single day

under Caligula. . . . Under Nero, four hundred tigers fought with bulls and elephants. . . . In a single day, at the dedication of the Collosseum by Titus, five thousand animals perished. Under Trajan, the games continued for one hundred and twenty-three consecutive days. Lions, tigers, elephants, rhinoceroses, hippopotami, giraffes, bulls, stags, even crocodiles and serpents were employed to give novelty to the spectacle. Nor was any form of human suffering wanting. . . . Ten thousand men fought during the games of Trajan. Nero illuminded his gardens by night by Christians burning in their pitchy shirts. Under Domitian, an army of feeble dwarfs was compelled to fight. . . . So intense was the craving for blood, that a prince was less unpopular if he neglected the distribution of corn than if he neglected the games.[31]

It is not that the Romans were without moral sentiment; rather, because animals were outside the sphere of moral concern, the Roman attitude was that anything goes. How can the nonvegetarian consistently object to these Roman practices regarding animals? Only on the grounds that it is good to save endangered species? And why save them? For *human* pleasure?

Against this sort of cultural background, it is surprising that vegetarianism survived at all in the Roman Empire. But, as shown, Seneca expressed concern for the suffering of animals, and Ovid was a vegetarian who especially upheld a belief both in the golden age (see chapter 2) and transmigration. Thus, in the fifteenth book of the *Metamorphoses* he states: "Alas what wickedness to swallow flesh into our own flesh, to fatten our greedy bodies by cramming in other bodies, to have one living creature fed by the death of another!"[32] Although animals fell within the sphere of Ovid's moral concern, one reason they were not generally so perceived was that not even many humans were considered of moral worth. The Christian Emperor Justinian's codification of Roman law holds that although slaves cannot be outraged by punishment themselves, their masters can be outraged *through* the slave. With this in mind, it should not be surprising that animals also had only a vicarious sentiency, which was even felt by so hardy a Stoic as Cicero.[33]

Williams pays particular attention to Ovid, because Ovid's concern for the golden age unifies vegetarian theory from the eighth-century Orphics to the Roman period.[34] For Williams, Ovid is also a descendant of Hesiod and Pythagoras, the founders of antikreophagy (*kreophagos* = eating flesh); the Pythagorean community spread across the Mediterranean world both geographically and temporally. According to Williams, vegetarianism as a social revolution had a communal foundation in ancient Greece; the prohibition against killing animals was the glue that held the commune together. Although this prohibition was spiritual at first, vegetarians gradually became aware of the humanitarian roots of their position—"humanitarianism" being defined by Williams as "the extension of the sublime principles of justice and compassion to all harmless sentient existence, irrespective of nationality, creed, or species." This communal bond between Pythagoras and Ovid also helps explain Pythagorean abstinence from beans: the bean, being used as an instrument to cast votes in the ballot, was employed by Pythagoras to symbolically dissuade his followers from "participating in the idle strife of party faction." Empedocles was also a member of the commune, albeit an aristocratic member who threw his support with the poor, calling attention to the political overtones of the vegetarian message. Plato, "the second founder of Pythagoreanism," brings the ideas of vegetarianism and community together in the *Republic*, the second book of which is a veiled defense of vegetarianism (see chapter 4). It is this tradition—which reigned supreme in the golden age—with which Ovid explicitly identifies himself.

In addition to Ovid, the remarkable Plutarch flourished in the first two centuries A.D. He was a Greek priest at Delphi, a position that put him in contact with the most ancient Greek traditions, including, as Gorman says, the Pythagorean stance regarding abstinence from beans.[35] Barrow may be correct when he says that Plutarch may have been more sympathetic to animals than *any* other Greek writer; Lecky would agree, claiming that Plutarch was the first to advocate vegetarianism on grounds of universal benevolence.[36] This may or may not be the case, but it is true that Plutarch defended vegetarianism on grounds other than transmigration. Even when his two-year-old daughter died, Plutarch restrained himself from believing that she would return.[37] His vegetarianism, above all others in antiquity, was anything but eccentric.[38] This will become apparent in the following treatment of several texts from his *Moralia* which deal with animals.[39]

Plutarch must have been influenced by Plato in his "Account of the Laws and Customs of the Lacedaemonians," the most famous group of which were the Spartans. The most ancient of these people were vegetarian, but even their meat-eating successors showed moderation by eating only a bit of flesh in their soups at the common table (1–2). Further, the Lacedaemonians prepared their bodies for food with hard work, and were careful not to pamper themselves with a frivolous diet; manliness was shown in the ability to endure fasting (3).

One of the chief difficulties in maintaining this sort of regimen is described in "Rules for the Preservation of Health." This is the temptation one faces when invited to a house where vegetarianism or moderation are not practiced (4), a praxic difficulty faced by all contemporary vegetarians as well. Plutarch holds Socrates as an exemplar here, for Socrates advised one not to eat unless hungry (6)—as Xenophon noted. Although Socrates was apparently not a vegetarian, he would nonetheless disapprove of eating certain meats (e.g., udder) that are eaten only to incite men to do rare things (not to mention the terrible pain this delicacy must have caused the animal). Plutarch's contemporaries must have been oblivious to what was a Lacedaemonian commonplace: rare and noble dishes are obtained only from acts of violence committed on nature;[40] we receive more honor from abstaining than from eating such dishes. In addition to Socrates, Plutarch favorably cites Crates (see chapter 4), a Cynic philosopher who seems to be an honorary Lacedaemonian for his refusal to go beyond a lentil in his meals.

The scent of meat, Plutarch thinks, is like an itch that, when scratched, needs more scratching (7). A healthy body does not need meat or any other excess food, exhibited by the fact that those who dine with Plato (or Crates) never complain the morning after (9), although they may have gluttonously complained the night of the meal. Meat, like wine, has an inebriating effect on the body (12). It should be remembered that in this piece on "Rules for the Preservation of Health," Plutarch often speaks as an ancient scientist, not always as a philosopher. For example, to properly remove human waste we must be careful to avoid those foods—like meat—which the body has difficulty releasing (18). It would be best to eat no flesh at all, but inasmuch as custom (*ethos*) is almost second nature, people do eat flesh, endangering health and psychic well-being (18). This reluctant capitulation to custom (much like Pythagoras's relaxation of rules for the *akousmatikoi*) should not be confused with Plutarch's own position, which is consistently vegetarian.[41] One last point from this essay should be noted: Plutarch suggests that sentiency is a matter of degree when he compares the life of an oyster with that of a tree (23). Interestingly enough, Singer's utilitarian position—built on the sentiency of higher animals, and not on their rationality—forces him to moderate his case as he moves "down" the evolutionary scale:

> Those who want to be absolutely certain that they are not causing suffering will not eat mollusks . . . but somewhere between a shrimp and an oyster is as good a place to draw the line as any, and better than most.[42]

In "The Banquet of the Seven Wise Men" Plutarch recalls the position of Solon, who holds, along with Hesiod and Pythagoras, that mallow and asphodel are some of the best foods.[43] By eating these and other useful vegetal foods, we are not just offering a pretense for a Tartuffe-like moral aristocracy, but we are really avoiding injuring or killing animals (cf., *Works and Days*, 41). If a man must harm a being in order to subsist, the fault is divine, not human. This is clearly not the usual case with one who eats meat. Meat is hardly a necessity, either in our modern world or in the ancient one.

Plutarch continues his reverence for previous "vegetarian" thinkers in "According to Epicurus." Along with Metrodorus, Epicurus considers avoiding evil (pain) to be the very essence and consummation of good. Epicurus did not consider himself superior to animals in at least one respect: neither he nor animals had any legitimate ideas about the gods (8). Although this position seems to allow for the possibility that killing an animal could be just as evil (and painful) as killing a human being, Epicurus remained vegetarian only in practice and not in theory, as was suggested earlier. In a way, the vegetarian as a social outcast has little pride and takes whatever support he can get. Plutarch would agree with Epicurus that most men (i.e., meat eaters) draw out the dimensions of their pleasures like a circle, with the stomach as the center; their prime interest lies in their belly (16, 17).

In several of "The Roman Questions," Plutarch elaborates what is obvious to the vegetarian but seldom noticed by others: eating is a serious matter that we often take for granted (Q. 64); e.g., we often fail to notice the similarity between raw meat and a raw wound (Q. 110). Plutarch's purpose is not to arouse pity, but to remind those who eat flesh without having witnessed the animal's death that their fare succumbed to the edge of a knife. Too often, he seems to suggest, we assume that what we eat was created *ex nihilo* and put in a cellophane wrapper.

Plutarch's vegetarianism is part of an overall view of the cosmos, a view he thinks was originated by Pythagoras. In "The Sentiments of Nature Philosophers Delighted In," Plutarch reminds us that several philosophers (in fact, all except Democritus, Epicurus, and their followers) have believed that the world itself is besouled and animallike (chaps. I, III). Within this universe there are animals per se, which have been variously viewed (chap. XX): Democritus and Epicurus only consider heavenly animals as rational; Anaxagoras endows animals with reason, albeit an inferior reason; Pythagoras and Plato ac-

cept animals as rational *simpliciter*, with only their bodies pre-
venting them from exhibiting a discursive reason; and Diogenes
sees animals as possessing a defective reason like that of a
madman.

Disagreements have also arisen regarding plants (chap. XXVI).
Plato and Empedocles believe that plants are animals—but Plutarch must here be referring to the "third" type of soul in the
Timaeus (see chapter 4). Aristotle thinks plants are alive, but
are obviously not animals, whereas the Stoics and Epicureans
do not even think of plants as besouled. Observe that even on
Platonic grounds there are notable differences between plants
and animals. Earlier men, perhaps those in the golden age,
must have realized this (chap. XXVII).

In his "Symposiacs" Plutarch returns to the matter of health
that he treated in "Rules for the Preservation of Health." Superfluous dainties neglect the necessary conditions for health (Bk.
IV, Q. 1), and health could be more easily obtained if we ate a
simple, unvaried diet. Appealing again to Socrates, Plutarch
makes us aware of how difficult it is to become a vegetarian in a
culture that "forces" its many options on us. But the vegetarian,
Plutarch seems to say, can always find a meatless item on the
menu if he tries. Plutarch realizes that his thesis regarding the
simplicity of food is a bland, so to speak, suggestion. However,
even if one believes that a variety of foods is healthy, the vegetarian can offer a cornucopia of delights, as Plato noticed when
he described the food of the Republic.

At another point in the "Symposiacs" Plutarch supplements
the efforts of the Pythagoreans by scientifically discussing why
certain foods are appetite stimulants or depressants (Bk. VI, Q.
2). He asks why hunger is allayed by drinking, but thirst is in-
creased by eating (Q. 3). Although the details of these queries
are not of much interest to me, it is important to note that Plutarch's vegetarianism, built on philosophical grounds to be examined shortly, constitutes a research program designed to
show why certain foods can be considered healthy, especially
those obtained without killing animals. I use the word "especially" here because Plutarch makes it clear that meat-eating de-

pends on a wrongful, violent slaughtering of animals (Q. 4). That is, sanctions against eating particular foods do not necessarily rest on superstitious grounds, but can arise out of a respect for at least all highly sentient beings.

Finally, before moving to the key texts in Plutarch, I should call attention to Plutarch's awareness of the Egyptian tradition of vegetarianism in "Of Isis and Osiris." The Egyptian priests knew that the earth bears enough edible fruit to allow us to decline the flesh of animals; Plutarch agrees with these priests that we ought to have regard for the brute beasts.

Plutarch's treatise "Of Eating the Flesh" in his *Moralia* is the only extant work from antiquity, except for Porphyry's *De abstinentia*, that deals primarily with philosophical vegetarianism. As may be suspected, this work is the most important one in Plutarch's corpus for my purposes. The persona of the "reader" in Plutarch's work wants to know why Pythagoras abstained from eating flesh, a question that offers Plutarch an excuse to develop his own position. He has a mocking admiration for the first man who ate animal flesh, thus presupposing that there was once a time of ancient perfection when flesh was not eaten. How could this man name the parts of meat that had shortly before lowed and cried? How could he smell the blood of flayed and mangled bodies? Plutarch asks such questions not for histrionic display, but rather to determine how such a monstrous act as unnecessarily killing an animal could have become so commonplace an event that it did not demand justification. The burden of proof for Plutarch (as for Regan and other contemporary vegetarians) is on the person who continues to kill, or who fuels the killing of animals by buying meat; it is not on the person who discontinues meat-eating (Tract I, 1).

The first meat eaters probably did what they did because of a scarcity of vegetal food, not because of lawless behavior. But the continued existence of meat eating leads Plutarch to bemoan, in Hesiodic fashion, the age into which he was born. Killing animals was a degenerate act mirrored in the chaos of nature itself in the post-golden ages: inundations of rivers, unfertile fields, and so on. Plutarch's era, however, although not one before the fall, nonetheless provided enough food to meet needs without polluting nature through spilling blood. The cruel irony is that it is man himself, defiled with blood, who calls other animals savage (2).[44]

Plutarch directly confronts the question of whether or not animals suffer (4). To determine this, we must first consider the evidence we have for determining whether human beings suffer (in Singer-like fashion). If a human being screamed and writhed when struck or bludgeoned, would one say he was in pain? Need he be articulate for one to conclude that he suffered? Of course not. Then how can we fancy that the screams of animals (with nervous systems like ours) are nothing but

> certain inarticulate sounds and noises, and not the several deprecations, entreaties, and pleadings of each of them, as it were saying thus to us: 'I deprecate not thy necessity (if such there be), but thy wantoness. Kill me for thy feeding, but do not take me for thy better feeding.' O horrible cruelty!

The clever meat eater at this point thinks about the possibility of killing the animal without pain. But precisely because of his sentiency the animal would still be deprived of something. Later, Plutarch will support his belief stated here (4) that animals are prudent (sunesei): "But for the sake of some little mouthful of flesh we deprive a soul of the sun and light, and of that proportion of life and time it had been born into the world to enjoy." Animals not only suffer, but also anticipate their sufferings, as is indicated by their fearful reactions to the smell of other animals' blood at the slaughterhouse.[45] And if animals anticipate, which even Aristotle would grant, they have a future of some sort. Thus, killing an animal painlessly (which is rare in modern slaughterhouses) would still be denying it "that proportion of life and time it had been born into the world to enjoy." And animals do enjoy themselves, as can be seen in the playful gambols of a hen in a yard. One should look, by way of contrast, at the modern henhouse, which is usually kept dark (N.B., Plutarch's reference to sunlight) so its inhabitants do not see their predicament—i.e., debeaked so they do not peck their fellows or themselves to death out of frustration with their crowded conditions; when a door is opened, and the chickens see a shaft of light, pandemonium breaks loose. Yet some would suppose that animals have no anticipation, hence no right to a future.[46]

The remarkably contemporary sound of Plutarch's arguments is just as apparent when he says that

> it is truly an affecting sight to see the very table of rich people laid before them . . . with dead corpses for their daily fare; but it is yet more affecting to see it taken away, for the mammocks left are more than that which was eaten. These therefore were slain to no purpose. [4]

Inasmuch as Plutarch points out that this is an activity of the rich, he seems to be suggesting that not only is this activity harmful to animals, but it also seems to deny something to the poor.

Although Plutarch does not intertwine his philosophical arguments with considerations of transmigration, he does mix them with matters of health (5). He holds that evidence for the unnaturalness of eating flesh comes from the human body, which lacks the characteristics of ravenousness that carnivores —who eat other animals of necessity—have, e.g., sharp incisors. His thought experiment is intended to be instructive: if you want to eat flesh, kill the animal yourself without the aid of a weapon, as lions do, who kill and eat at once. Plutarch would have us notice that fruits can be eaten much more naturally (although it is difficult to imagine agriculture developing without "unnatural" tools). Further, because we cannot eat meat immediately after the kill (i.e., "naturally") as carnivores do, we must preserve it with seasonings as though we were embalming the flesh.

No one but a Cynic would eat raw flesh to prove Plutarch's point; this is precisely what Diogenes did when he tried raw fish and other flesh (6), an act that weakened Diogenes' mind, according to Plutarch.[47] He sees Diogenes as bestial, but at least he is an honest beast who does not cover up his bestiality as do most meat eaters. As illustrated in earlier chapters, the case of Diogenes is a peculiar one. Boas saw Diogenes as an admirer of animals, and not only because he lived like a dog (cynos).[48] For Boas, Diogenes was in search of that life most in accord with nature, and animals seemed even more natural than barbaric peoples like the Scythians. All human beings are controlled by some law, and law is a convention and not natural, because "natural" to the Cynic meant untouched or uncorrupted. When Diogenes saw a dog lapping water from a puddle, he realized that cups were superfluous; likewise with clothes that did more than protect him from the elements like an animal's fur.[49] Because beasts had no need of houses, Diogenes crept into a wine jar; also, beasts ate their food raw, so why cook? Even cannibalism was wrongly censured. None of this showed that animals were worthy of respect, or that they were rational; and even if they were rational, reason was of doubtful value for Diogenes. But following an animallike way of life increases one's autonomy (autarchy), even if it did make one "bestial."[50] The point Plutarch wants to make is that the meat eater *ought* to have the courage and candid attitude of Diogenes (if, in fact, Diogenes had this attitude), but does not.

Far worse than the Cynic is the one who would torture a live animal; this man is even worse than one who kills the animal for food. In that both practices are allowed by custom, few men object to them, although the torture of animals is usually only tolerated when it is of some benefit to man, to the chagrin of the antivivesectionist.[51] In fact, there is a story from antiquity of Xenocrates being fined for skinning a ram alive.[52]

Tract II in "Of Eating the Flesh" reveals Plutarch's frustration, for it is difficult to dispute with men's bellies, which are custombound with an enchantment as strong as that of Circe: "Of groans and frauds and sorcery replete."[53] Human beings, like fish, are hooked with their own luxurious eating habits. As previously seen, Plutarch proves to be no ironclad dilettante in his willingness to compromise with his opponent:

Let us at least sin with discretion. Let us eat flesh; but let it be for hunger and not for wantoness. Let us kill an animal; but let us do it with sorrow and pity, and not abusing and tormenting it, as many nowadays are used to do, while some run red-hot spits through the bodies of swine, that by the tincture of the quenched iron the blood may be to that degree mortified, that it may sweeten and soften the flesh in its circulation; others jump and stamp upon the udders of sows that are ready to pig, that so they may trample into one mass, in the very pangs of delivery, blood, milk, and the corruption of the crushed and mangled young ones, and so eat the most inflamed part of the animal; others sew up the eyes of cranes and swans, and so shut them up in darkness to be fattened, and then souse up their flesh with certain monstrous mixtures and pickles.

Before the reader excuses such practices as historically unique to ancient insensitivity, he should realize that contemporary techniques are hardly less vicious: veal calves are practically starved before their slaughter so as to keep their meat the shade of pink consumers like; and the cosmetics so "essential" to modern beauty may have caused great pain to rabbits and cats.[54]

The above passage makes three points clear: (1) because it is not necessary to eat flesh, we ought to avoid causing unnecessary suffering, a point Porphyry especially noticed about Plutarch's theory;[55] (2) if human beings "must" eat flesh, such eating should at least be done reluctantly and when hungry—this is Plutarch's compromise; and (3) if one eats flesh or uses animals *only* for luxury or taste, no sort of apology can be offered—no compromise can be made! Plutarch's uneasiness regarding point (2) illustrates his difficulty in distinguishing it from point (3). That is, his compromise may be compromising. But such is the price the vegetarian must pay in order to avoid the charge of dogmatism from his (open-minded?) meat-eating opponent, who is more than willing to ridicule the vegetarian as a fanatic.

The villainy of those who kill animals for luxury is analogous to those who cannot satiate their intemperance upon women (2). And what meal is not luxurious?, Plutarch might be asked. Strictly speaking, that for which no animal is put to death. But we have seen that Plutarch is realistic in his reading of the *zeitgeist*. How can a soul be worthless that can feel (*aistheseos*), see, hear, imagine (*phantasias*), think (*suneseos*), search for what is agreeable, and avoid what is disagreeable? Plutarch believes that animals possess all of these qualities, for they are intelligent pleasure-seekers. There is nothing new about this position, so far as Plutarch is concerned, for it was also the view of Pythagoras and Empedocles, and before them of the ancient Greeks themselves (3).

Exactly who was it that first said we owe no justice to dumb animals? "Who first beat out accursed steel, and made the lab'ring ox a knife to feel?" (4). Plutarch does not know who the individual was, but he thinks he understands the process. In the beginning some wild and mischievous beast was killed (and eaten), giving some degree of pleasure to the killer; then an ox, a bird, etc., until little by little, "unsatiableness being strengthened by use," men would not stop at anything. Plutarch makes this conjecture from historical evidence regarding the killing of men within Greek society. The first man the Athenians ever put to death was the basest of knaves, yet eventually even the philosopher Polemarchus (not to mention Socrates) suffered death.[56] Plutarch holds that killing animals, whether human or not, is a savage and intemperate habit which inclines the mind more brutishly to bloodshed and destruction. This argument seems to link the issues of capital punishment and meat-eating. The Greeks practiced both, the latter to the point where it was virtually impossible to entertain friends or invite guests to a wedding without blood and slaughter. Anything less would not be "civilized."

Plutarch's attitude toward transmigration deserves some attention (5); he uses what I call an analogous argument from uncertainty. Suppose one were in a night battle and came upon a fallen, yet living, body that one thought might be a son or

brother. Would it be better to ignore the fallen body, thus running the risk that it was an enemy soldier, or to kill it, running
the risk that it was a relative?[57] The former, of course. Likewise,
if a sheep stands before us with inclined neck, and one person
tells us it is nothing but an unreasoning animal, while another
that there may be a soul of a friend or god in the beast, we have
a practical imperative to believe the latter. Two things should
be noted about this approach: (1) Plutarch does not base his
vegetarian position on a belief in transmigration in any direct
way, as do some previous Greek vegetarians (although they, too,
had other arguments). Plutarch's certainty regarding vegetarianism and the tentativeness of his belief in transmigration shows
that the two positions are theoretically distinct. And (2), even if
transmigration is outmoded, this *sort* of argument could still
have some force. For example, if one suspects that it *might* be
wrong to cause unnecessary suffering or death, and such suffering or death could be easily avoided, then there may be a practical imperative to "play it safe." This would force the opponent
of vegetarianism into something close to dogmatic assurance if
he wanted his case to stand. Having put his opponent into this
uncomfortable position, Plutarch ends his essay, which must be
considered a classic by the philosophic vegetarian.[58]

Two dialogues of Plutarch are also worthy of consideration.
The first asks, "Which are the Most Crafty, Water or Land Animals?," and deals with far more serious topics than one might
suspect. Against the voluptuous appetites of the hunter, one of
the participants commends the Pythagoreans (2) for their humanity and compassion (*philanthropou kai philoiktirmou*), for
inculcating into men a mild and gentle care of beasts.[59] The
Pythagorean position, however, receives opposition from the
Stoic portico (3): just as immortal is the opposite of mortal, reasonable beings are the opposite of irrational beings, including
animals. This seems an illegitimate opposition, however, even
on Stoic grounds where everything in the *cosmos* is pervaded
by reason (*logos*). Nor should a rigid distinction be made (à la
Aristotle) between sensation and reason; sense affords all who
are capable of it a "knowledge" of what is useful and hurtful. Or

at least sensation provides a necessary condition for rationality, for if an animate being is deprived of expectation, memory, fear, desire, and the like, he can hardly understand the world around him. It may also be the case, if Plutarch is pushed, that sensation is a sufficient condition for rationality or understanding (noein); but this is by no means clear in the text, and would be a difficult position to maintain. Punishment of dogs and horses affirms, in a practical way, the intimate link between sense and reason, otherwise the animal would not understand why he was being hit. Also, to punish an animal indicates that the animal can feel, and not just feel "as it were." To say the latter (the position of Cartesian speciesism) would be as strange as saying that animals as it were see, or as it were live. If we cannot say that they see, live, or feel, how can we say that human beings do these things?

The Stoic and his allies must therefore be accused of duplicity. They assert that love of parents toward children (philostorgian) is a virtue, then view the same emotion in animals but deny it as a virtue (4). Yet, strangely enough, animals have such vices as maliciousness which allows us to punish them. If the suggestion is that animals do not have the highest degree of reason and virtue and hence we need not be just to them, then one should consider whether many (or any) human beings have these attributes preeminently. A being with poor sight can still see. A man can still be strong even if he lacks the strength of a camel (4, 5). But the beast must always be attacked when the vegetarian is near. Antipater found fault with the dirtiness of sheep, yet ignored the lynx, who always hides his excrement (4).

Both Plutarch and Porphyry note that there is a defect to every faculty (5).[60] An eye can succumb to blindness, but that which is not naturally adapted to see cannot be blind. Therefore—as Porphyry holds in his interpretation of Plutarch—an animal cannot be delirious or mad unless intellection (dianoeisthai) and the discursive energy of reason (logizesthai) are naturally inherent. But even if animals are rational, Stoics and some Peripatetics would claim because they cannot be just to us, we have no duty to be just to them (6). The aforementioned argument from marginal cases, however, can meet this objection, because many human beings are not sufficiently rational to be just to others. Then again, the prevalence of infanticide in ancient Greece offers the meat eater an escape, though hardly one that can hold its own today. Or if it can hold its own, at least one can show the extraordinary lengths to which the meat eater must go to make his case. That is, when confronted with the argument from marginal cases—which in effect says that *if* we have duties to infants, those in comas, or the mentally defective (i.e., marginal cases of humanity), *then* we have duties to the higher animals as well—the ancient Greek opponent to vegetarianism may well have denied that we have a responsibility toward marginal cases of humanity.

Plutarch wants to corner philosophers who eat meat (7), especially those who take their eating habits for granted. And he thinks that there is historical support for his "aggressiveness": both Empedocles *and* Heraclitus believed that man could not be totally exonerated in dealing with beasts as he "now" does. Obviously Pythagoras is also cited, but with a new wrinkle: he shows us how to reap benefits from animals without being unjust, e.g., by taming those that are capable of being gentle and making them our assistants, for as Plutarch quotes Aeschylus:

> The horse and ass, that backs to load resign,
> And race of bulls,
> Kind Heaven vouchsafed to men by toil distrest,
> With servile limbs his labors to assist.

Life does not end if we do not eat a calf's liver; perhaps we could survive even if we only exercised the calf. But even here there are dangers: one might be tempted to exercise and work animals in a detrimental way (7) in the greedy attempt to make money—e.g., with drugged race horses, and the like.

Section 8 of this dialogue introduces several hunters who make a case for the superiority of land animals over water animals, thereby attempting to answer the question in the title of the work. Without realizing the consequences of their admissions, these hunters agree with all of the attributes given to land animals by Autobulus and Soclarus (the Plutarchians). The more they praise animals, the more they unwittingly support the vegetarian's case. Architecture, future-oriented reasoning, artifice (10), friendship, continence, justice, reason (contra Cleanthes), and equity (11) are all possessed by various animals. Aristodemus, one of the hunters, even goes to the extreme by showing compassion for the ant whose hill is dug up by the scientist (11); perhaps here Plutarch is offering a caricature of his own position. In his *Life of Pericles* (1) Plutarch makes it clear that he does not approve of squandering love and affection, which are due primarily to human beings, on animals (poodle-mania?). Animals are not to be worshipped, as Clark notices, if for no other reason than a primitive worship of animals often leads to their sacrifice.[61]

Animals are even capable of syllogistic deduction, as seen in the case of the fox who, treading gently, lays his ear to the ice to perceive the noise of water, thereby reasoning that the ice is too thin to cross. Exquisiteness of sense, the hunter holds, fails to explain how animals can do such things (13).

Phaedimus, a fisherman, rises to defend the water animals (23), whose virtues and intelligence are greater than that of land animals, a fact which is hidden because of our failure to discern what inhabits the sea-depths. Fish know the cunning of fishermen, show affection (24), know the equinoxes (29), have a mutual society, love their young (32), and the like. Barrow notes that Plutarch's remarks on the dolphin (36) anticipate current research on this animal.[62] Only the dolphin, the fisherman holds, loves man unconditionally.

The conclusion of the dialogue makes it clear that Plutarch has avoided fabulous stories to the extent that he can, and has reported only what men have actually seen animals do. Soclarus acquits both sides in this dispute, and surprises them by declaring the hunters and fishermen champions *against* those who would deprive animals of sense and understanding (37).

"That Brute Beasts Make Use of Reason" has an obvious theme, but the most unusual format. This piece is also a dialogue, but the participants are Odysseus, Circe, and Gryllus, a man who was turned into a pig by Circe. Barrow correctly points out the Cynic influence on this piece, as it was a Cynic commonplace to wrap a lesson in satiric form.[63] Odysseus wants to restore men like Gryllus to their human form, pitying them in their present shape. Gryllus will have nothing of this, for he thinks that men are the most miserable of creatures. Animals are superior to men, he thinks, because they bear spontaneous virtue just as a paradisal (golden) land would bear fruit. For example, animals are naturally courageous, whereas human fortitude is akin to prudent fear, a knowing timidity which forces man to do one thing to avoid another. Furthermore, animals do not lust for wealth, exhibiting a temperance men should aim for; female animals attract their males with their own scents, but women corrupt themselves with perfume; beasts are not adulterers; and finally, men have forced themselves sexually on beasts, but never the other way around. Plutarch is having a grand time here, with at least some justification. When one conjures up the image of a man having intercourse with a sheep, it is difficult to believe the traditional line about the inferiority of nonhuman animals.

Perhaps more important, man is the only all-devourer (*pamphagon*). Animals abstain from all or most animals, are at enmity with only a few, and eat only when compelled by hunger. Man, with a plentiful supply of herbs, fruits, and vegetables "must" try them all. The natural instinct of animals is denigrated by some, but nature is hardly a teacher to be criticized, Gryllus suggests, when one sees the incredible behavior of human beings. The dialogue ends with Odysseus thoroughly whipped, finally resting his case on the human ability to know the gods; Gryllus's last sentence breaks off as he appropriately refers to Sisyphus.

Cynic influences can be perceived in this dialogue along with inverted echoes of Aristophanes' *Clouds* (1427–29), where Pheidippides uses the example of cocks to justify beating his father.[64] The New Comedy was also fond of portraying the unnaturalness of human behavior in contrast to that of animals. Pliny, in Plutarch's own century, wonders whether nature is man's kindly parent or cruel stepmother.[65] What folly, he thinks, to hold that man is born to a high estate! Man alone may know the gods, but man alone worries about his fate at the hands of the gods. None of this was lost on some later thinkers, especially skeptics like Montaigne.[66] Unfortunately, as was suggested in chapter 1, this praise of animals was not carried over into *praxis* in the thought of later skeptics as it was in the more direct, powerful analysis of Plutarch. There is a deceptive simplicity to his thought that may prevent the more "sophisticated" contemporary reader from appreciating the ease with which Plutarch can *act* as a vegetarian without endlessly searching for an *apologia* for his humanity.

6　THE NEOPLATONISTS

ALTHOUGH not at all influenced by Neoplatonism, Singer defends himself against an imagined charge long directed at the Neoplatonists: impracticality. As he puts it,

> Becoming a vegetarian is not merely a symbolic gesture. Nor is it an attempt to isolate oneself from the ugly realities of the world, to keep oneself pure and so without responsibility for the cruelty and carnage all around. . . . So long as people are prepared to buy the products of intensive farming, the usual forms of protest and political action will never bring about a major reform.[1]

Well put. But Stephen Clark, a major figure in the recent revival of vegetarian thought who would agree with Singer's remark, *does* explicitly identify himself with Neoplatonism, although, as Benson notices, Clark does not always argue for his Neoplatonic stance.[2] In *The Moral Status of Animals*, Clark only considers himself a Neoplatonist on Thursdays (p. 5); his occasional Neoplatonism, however, supports a full-time vegetarianism, hinted at in these words:

> We are not separate from the world, nor are we its masters: if men have an office "higher" than those of other creatures

it is the office of care and understanding—understanding of cosmic *unity*, care for the *diversity* of creatures. [My emphasis; pp. 194–95]

Clark's position, like Neoplatonism, is not naive, however. He realizes that the belief that the phenomenal world is an expression of a spiritual reality can be dangerous to animals, in that it might be assumed that one could kill and eat a cow as long as one revered Cowness (p. 64). This bastardized Neoplatonism is kept alive, quite ironically, in some meat eaters' appreciation of pastoral painting and poetry, where The Bird, The Fish, et al., are painted or described with an archetypal, reverential awe, while individual birds or fish in reality are easily killed and eaten. All we notice about individual pigs is that they are tokens of the type Pig. Neoplatonism realizes that often spirit is divided against itself, and not in a Gnostic or Manichean way, as is evidenced by the fact that Plotinus attacked the Manichees as fiercely as St. Augustine (pp. 194, 19).

The popularity of vegetarianism among the Neoplatonists attests to its practicality, if not its rationality. From what Haussleiter calls the early Neoplatonists (like Apollonius of Tyana in the first century A.D.) to the end of the classical period, vegetarianism received new life, a mini-rising of the phoenix rivaling the enthusiasm of the days of Pythagoras. I will focus on two of these figures—Plotinus and Porphyry—but it should be remembered that dotting the landscape are many minor figures whose names and positions we hardly know. Phoclydes, Hierocles, and the like are hardly household names even in classical circles; Iamblichus, a student of Porphyry whose *Life of Pythagoras* was mentioned in an earlier chapter, is a bit more well known; and seminal Proclus in the fifth century, although not as rigorous a vegetarian as Porphyry, seems to have adopted the practice. As Gorman points out, the tradition of philosophical vegetarianism endured in some form or another until Justinian closed the Academy in the sixth century, ending (albeit temporarily) a 1,000-year-old intellectual history.[3] In chapter 1, I suggested why vegetarianism was discontinued in the "Christian" age, but since then we have seen that Christianity was, in part, revising certain Greek attitudes toward animals. Porphyry and other philosophical vegetarians might nonetheless hold that Peripatetics, Stoics, and Christians *ought* to have had different attitudes toward animals, even based on their own theories: the Peripatetics because of the features Aristotle himself attributes to animals (as noticed by Theophrastus); the Stoics because of the artificially rigid distinction between *logos endiathetios* and *logos prophorikos* (see chapter 5, n. 78); and the Christians because of the primacy in their religion of *agape* (which does not demand love in return) and concern for the suffering of others. With only a slight touch of smugness, the modern vegetarian can gain some solace from considering the fact that Plotinus and Porphyry did what they were "supposed" to do.

It is certain that Plotinus was a vegetarian, although it takes a little work to determine why. In his *Life of Plotinus*, Porphyry clearly states that Plotinus did not approve of eating the flesh of animals reared for the table, nor would he even accept medicine made from animals (2). We are not told why Plotinus held these beliefs, but given our knowledge of Pythagorean vegetarianism, and the known influence of the Pythagorean tradition on Plotinus, some reasonable inferences can be made, the most noteworthy of which is that Plotinus seemed to be ashamed of being "in the body" (1). His was the contemplative life; he never relaxed from his interior musings except when asleep. Food seemed only a reluctantly taken necessity, crucial to continue his existence as a contemplator. He lived a regime of abstinence, and recommended the same to other philosophers (7–8). This evidence seems to imply that Plotinus's vegetarianism was largely due to his asceticism, and to his desire for spiritual perfection. Also, because Plotinus came from Egypt he may have encountered Oriental varieties of vegetarianism, as was the case with Pythagoras. After leaving his teacher, Ammonius Saccas, Plotinus joined the expeditionary army of Gordian and traveled to another cosmopolitan area, Persia. Scholars like Brehier (cf., Armstrong) insist upon the importance of Oriental influences on Plotinus's thought.[4]

Perhaps Plotinus's vegetarianism can be more accurately perceived by considering the *Enneads* themselves. (1) It must be noted that Plotinus remarks several times that human souls can be reincarnated in the bodies of animals, reminding one of an Orphic-Pythagorean commonplace.[5] (2) Plotinus apparently deduces the appropriateness of vegetarianism from the tripartite Aristotelian division of soul, à la Theophrastus. Whereas plants have no feeling,[6] and hence cannot suffer, animals *can* feel pleasure and pain.[7] What differentiates man from other animals is not the ability to suffer (*pathein*), but the ability to consciously apprehend intellectual principles and look toward the One.[8] This superiority allows man to use animals in many ways (e.g., in farming),[9] but not to the point where animals must suffer unnecessarily. Plotinus's refusal to use medicines that come from animals may be due not so much to a primitive conception of medicine as to a concern for animals themselves. As a precursor to the modern antivivesectionist, Plotinus may not want to jump too quickly on the claim of "necessity" when causing pain to an animal; have all other attempts at gaining health been exhausted first? Plotinus might find it incredible to learn that in a nation still enjoying its fetish with cigarettes, millions of animals are killed each year on the "modern altars of Asclepius" so as to find a cure for cancer.[10] Pain, for Plotinus, is the perception (*aisthesis*) of the body despoiled, and is only experienced by sensitive beings like animals and humans. For example, amputation can be felt (and in some cases, anticipated) just as intensely in animals as in humans, due to the nonmaterial condition of sensitive soul in each. The human capacity to sympathize, Plotinus seems to say, should make us feel *pathos* for any victim upon whom unnecessary suffering is inflicted.[11]

And (3) Plotinus returns, in a way, to the myth of the golden age (see chapter 2). The *One* is symbolized by primeval Ouranos, *Intellect* by the golden age under Cronus, and *Soul* by the derivative ages under the rule of Zeus.[12] This playful use of myth may be seen as a veiled exhortation for all intellectual beings to return to the vegetarianism of that supposed golden age under Cronus.

It is no small pleasure to save the best until last. Without a doubt, the most comprehensive and subtly reasoned treatment of vegetarianism by an ancient philosopher is Porphyry's *De abstinentia*, the only extant work that deals precisely with the topic from antiquity in addition to Plutarch's "Of Eating the Flesh." It is a tribute to the richness of *De abstinentia* that there is still something to say about it, for I have referred to it so much in earlier chapters—especially regarding the argument from marginal cases in chapter 5 as a criticism of Stoicism. The text itself has played its own part in the history of animal rights. The English translator of the work, Thomas Taylor, borrowed from Porphyry in his 1792 book, *A Vindication of the Rights of Brutes*, which is not a panegyric to the brutes but an acerbic reply to Mary Wollstonecraft's *A Vindication of the Rights of Women*. Taylor suggests that if women are given rights, eventually *even* the beasts will receive them, thereby, he thinks, reducing the women's case to absurdity. The fact that Taylor's (at times misleading) translation is still in use indicates the need for classicists to become familiar with modern vegetarianism, especially now that women *do* have rights.[13]

Like his teacher Plotinus, Porphyry was a vegetarian. The occasion for the book is the defection from the ranks of vegetarianism of a fellow student of Plotinus in Rome, Firmus Castricius. Williams thinks that Firmus was lured away by the "fruits" of Christianity.[14] But it is unclear why he defected. Bouffartigue and Patillon (hereafter cited as BP) hold out the possibility that Firmus was opposed to patriotism, in that Porphyry wrote this work in Sicily, the ancient home of the Pythagoreans, where vegetarianism may still have contained political overtones.[15] In the final analysis, we just do not know why Firmus gave up vegetarianism. Being the encyclopaedist that he was, Porphyry wrote a work containing every possible reason why Firmus ought to remain vegetarian.[16] The work is divided into four books, each dealing with a different concern.

The first book deplores his friend's defection and treats the topic of moderation. Porphyry refuses to believe that Firmus makes his switch for reasons of health; only the vulgar (*idiotes*) would say that vegetarianism is unhealthy (2)! Rather, Firmus has deceived himself into thinking that vegetarianism makes no difference with respect to the acquisition of wisdom (*phronesin*). We should note that (Stoic?) indifference (*adiaphoria*) to the issue of vegetarianism is not only Firmus's problem, as Williams is quick to point out.[17] Porphyry starts to deal with the members of those antivegetarian traditions that may have led Firmus away: the Peripatetics, the Epicureans, and the Stoics. His objections to these traditions have been treated in previous chapters and will not be explored again here, where I am concerned primarily with how Porphyry develops his own position (3). For example, he makes it clear that unnecessary suffering must not be inflicted (11–12). Like Plutarch he realizes that dangerous animals and those which are redundant in the extreme (rats?) may have to be killed. Sheep and oxen, whose numbers are regulated by human beings, are not found in these categories.

A first century A.D. rhetorician, Claudius the Neopolitan, opposed vegetarianism and wrote a treatise against abstinence. Unfortunately, it is lost to us, except for Porphyry's summary of it (13–25). Apparently Claudius collected the common man's "arguments" against vegetarianism, with which Porphyry is concerned because he constantly notes the general absence of vegetarianism in the daily, mythological, and official life of culture (BP, vol. 1, p. lxvi). These common men (*polus kai demodes anthropos*) hold the following views: the ancients (in the golden age) abstained from meat not out of piety, but because they did not know how to use fire (13). Eating meat became natural only when men could cook their food, and when some people from every nation began to eat meat. There is an innate and just war (*polemos*) planted in us against brutes: some (lions and wolves) attack us voluntarily, some (snakes) only when trampled on. Other animals destroy the fruits of the earth. Therefore, we have a legitimate case against them. We can spare those animals that associate with us (dogs), but a hog is not useful (*chresimon*) for anything but food. Anyway, why should we abstain from eating animals (15)? Even animals eat animals, the most sagacious of which are hunters themselves. Eating flesh hinders neither soul nor body; in fact, athletes and physicians have testified to the healthiness of eating meat. Not only do we help ourselves by eating meat, we preserve ourselves against the takeover of our earth by those endlessly reproducing swine and hares (16), whose death will produce putrefied flesh which carries disease. Furthermore, one can legitimately ask how many men will not be cured if animals are not consumed (17); e.g., the blind are aided by eating vipers. And even if the case for abstention is a good one, does it not of necessity also apply to plants, thereby jeopardizing our very existence (18)? The vegetarian is an inconsistent thinker when one considers that he believes in transmigration yet refuses to eat meat, when this practice would liberate souls trapped in animals so that they could return to a human body all the more quickly (19). The meat eater can have his "cake" and eat it too: if animals are not worthy of respect we can kill them, and if they are worthy of respect (because they are frustrated human beings) we do them a favor by killing them (20). If the vegetarian persists, then he should also avoid milk, wool, and honey, for to use these would be stealing a calf's food, a sheep's vestment, and the bee's own nourishment (21). Even the gods demand animals to be killed (22–25). They have sense, for they realize that if animals were not killed, serpents would dominate the earth. And no more of the Pythagorean fiddle-faddle: killing and eating animals does *not* induce us to do the same to human beings.

The reader can see why Porphyry is indispensible for my topic. In addition to the previously cited objections of the Peripatetics, Epicureans,[18] and Stoics, he also gives us Claudius. That is, Porphyry's intellectual honesty leads him not only to offer the best possible reasons *for* vegetarianism, but also—and he considers it a duty—to collect the best reasons *against* it. Without him we would hardly know anything about Greek antivegetarian thought. The remarkably modern tenor of many of

Claudius's points encourages me to respond to him as if he were a contemporary: (1) It is purely conjecture on Claudius's part that primitive men were vegetarians because they lacked fire. (2) The cultural appropriation of nature found in the suggestion that it is natural to eat *cooked* flesh is part of a more general anthropocentrism that can be called into question.[19] (3) The fact that some people in all nations eat meat (if in fact this is true) does not in itself establish the legitimacy of meat-eating; to think otherwise is to stumble into the *argumentum ad populum*. (4) Porphyry is more than willing to admit that it is sometimes necessary to kill animals in order to save ourselves (e.g., Claudius's lions), but this does not support the case for an all-out war on animals, much less a just (*dikaios*) one.[20] (5) To see pigs only as "locomotor meals," as Clark puts it, denies them not only sentience but also the ability to associate with us; pigs have been known to be pets before.[21] "Graciously" elevating Claudius's arguments to the status of jewels, we might ask whether it is worthwhile to cast such swine before "pearls." Later we will see that Rorty's attitude toward pigs is no more sophisticated than Claudius's. (6) Although eating meat can be one of the sufficient conditions for a healthy diet, this does not establish the case, as Claudius thinks, for its being necessary. (7) It is not necessary for the vegetarian to build his case on transmigration; assuming that Porphyry accurately reports his arguments, Claudius fails to see that animals may be worthy of respect even if they are not really human or useful to humanity. Put simply, he is speciesist. (8) Claudius may well be correct, however, that the vegetarian should also be careful in his use of milk, wool, and honey, but not because of Claudius's supposed concern for theft. Rather, gathering these materials can (but does not necessarily) cause pain to the animals involved. (9) Obviously Claudius is correct that eating animals does not make us more likely to *eat* human beings; whether this applies to killing is open to doubt. And finally, (10) the issues of animals eating other animals, killing animals for cures, and the extension of the vegetarian's argument to plants have been treated before and need not detain us here.

Porphyry realizes that whatever he says will probably not convince those who are occupied in a life of labor, or those who are athletes, in that their standards are largely informed by tradition.[22] Rather, he would criticize Claudius or Firmus or others who have the time and inclination to consider how they ought to act and why (27); if they develop a body of *akousmatikoi* who can change tradition, all the better. Porphyry's overall goal is to obtain the contemplation of real being (29), which is obviously hindered in no mysterious way when human beings are fettered by the realization that they have killed sentient beings for no reason. Ignorance, of course, is bliss in that it can eliminate fetters. Dwelling in a foreign (i.e., meat-eating) land we seek an escape from barbarism (30) so that we may "enter the stadium naked and unclothed, striving for the most glorious of all prizes, the Olympia of the soul" (31). The point here is that pleasure and pain are the streams which irrigate the current by which the soul is linked to the body (32–34). For Porphyry, the soul is dyadic (unlike Plato's triad): (1) *nous* or *logos* is the rational part confronting (2) an irrational, passionate element (*alogon* or *pathetikon*—see BP, vol. 1, p. xlvii). To eat meat only because it tastes good is to delay our return to our "home," the road to which is paved with reason and restraint rather than with the Bacchic fury needed to slaughter animals. The goal is to transmute body into soul, not the other way around. The modern novelist Kazantzakis ably grasps Porphyry's point in the novel *Zorba the Greek*, where (the Dionysian) Zorba says to his (Neoplatonic) boss:

Tell me what you do with the food you eat, and I'll tell you who you are. Some turn their food into fat and manure, some into work and good humor, and others, I'm told, into God. So there must be three sorts of men. I'm not one of the worst, boss, nor yet one of the best. I'm somewhere between the two. What I eat I turn into work and good humor. . . . As for you, boss . . . I think you do your level best to turn what you eat into God. But you can't quite manage it, and that torments you.

To be purified of meat-eating is not easy (35), as it may require changing one's lifestyle, and avoiding those places where
a "hostile" crowd might ridicule vegetarianism. This is why
some Pythagoreans dwelt in solitary places (36), although even
in the cities there were sacred groves where solace could be
found. Plato's Academy was not far removed from the center
of things, yet Plato above all others knew of the seductive nature of a banquet (36–37). The irrational part of the soul, compared to the wayward steed of Plato's *Phaedrus*, is not capable
of judging which foods ought to be eaten; only the reasoning
charioteer is fit to judge (43–44). Today, it seems, this wild
horse goes under the name of "taste."

Reason, for Porphyry, rejects what is superfluous and circum-
scribes what is necessary within narrow boundaries (46). Modern vegetarians might learn from Porphyry that it is not their
job to show that one can still dine elegantly, although gourmet
vegetarian dishes often enable some to make the break with
meat more easily. Nearly every ancient philosopher (48), including some who were not vegetarian, preferred frugality—as
opposed to asceticism—to luxury. In this respect vegetarianism
was a quintessential Greek trait that acted as a paradigm (often
unrealized) for *all* Greeks. The "wealth" of nature is easily obtained, but that which proceeds from vain opinions is procured
with difficulty (49). Porphyry is not so much suggesting that
vegetarianism is more "natural" than other diets, but that flesh
consumption is a cultural phenomenon; eating meat is not built
into the structure of things as is the law of gravity. Nor does he
want to build his vegetarianism on half-baked scientific ideas.
The connection between vegetarianism and medicine is dependent on the connection between vegetarianism and philosophical reflection (50).[23] The multitude, however—that group defended not too altruistically by Claudius—will incessantly
labor to obtain more (steak?) even if their possessions are abundant (51). All to no avail. For Porphyry, variety of animal foods
does not even increase the pleasure of eating, much less its morality. This pleasure often enough is terminated as soon as pain
or desire is removed.

Our activities ought to follow a boundary or measure (54) such that the contemplative philosopher (*theoretikos*) is not even capable of desiring luxuries (56):

> For no one who can easily liberate himself from all pertur-
> bations, will desire to possess silver tables and couches,
> and to have ointments and cooks, splendid vessels and gar-
> ments, and suppers remarkable for their sumptuousness
> and variety; but such a desire arises from a perfect useless-
> ness to every purpose of the present life . . . and from im-
> mense perturbations. [55]

In short, adopting the language of Singer, animal liberation can also be human liberation, because our contest, for the Neoplato-nist, is for immortality and an association with divinity (56), an adhering to God as if fastened by a nail (57). Simplicity in eat-ing is a mirror of, above all else, the simplicity, purity, and self-sufficiency of the One.[24]

Book Two seems quite removed from present-day concerns in that it deals with the issue of animal sacrifices. Porphyry's point is that even if animals must be sacrificed, it does not follow that we should eat them (2, 44). This is the same sort of reasoning that applies to ferocious animals when they must be killed (4) and to human sacrifices as they have occurred in Greek history (53 ff.). Originally human beings sacrificed grass and the like (barley, honey, etc.), but when an ancient famine caused hard-ship, animals were called into service to placate the gods (5–9; see my treatment of Theophrastus in chapters 2 and 4).

Although Porphyry is tied to the religious beliefs of his age, one can sense his struggle to elevate religious discourse. The gods care more for the disposition or intention of those who sacrifice than for the sorts of things sacrificed (15). The Judeo-Christian tradition came to the same realization centuries be-fore, as is evidenced in the stories of Cain and Abel (where God accepted Abel's vegetal offerings), and where the poor woman gave "more" in Jesus' view than all others.

Clark sees even more significance in Book Two.[25] As he views it, all meat-eating is a corrupt application of symbolic processes. In Porphyry's day one's eating meat was connected with the symbols of subservience to the gods; in ours, meat-eating is symbolic of our supposed superior status in the world, our level of economic achievement, etc. Flesh-eating has been a metaphor, a sacrament, a secular feast; not to eat with one's fellows is often a denial of those symbols which cause consanguinity. For Porphyry a religious symbolism more appropriate than meat-eating is Quaker-like silence (33), a sacred sacrifice of our intellect, an offering of a pure soul (61).

Porphyry spends much of his time in this book with daemons, the souls of dead bodies, and the like. Yet even Voltaire realized that Porphyry's vegetarianism was not based on metempsychosis; and modern scholars at least recognize that metempsychosis is a difficult problem in Porphyry, not to be automatically alluded to in order to explain vegetarianism (BP, vol. 1, p. li).[26]

Book Three turns to a more familiar topic: justice. Vegetarianism is conducive not only to moderation (Book One) and piety (Book Two), but also to justice. To extend justice to animals, Passmore holds that Porphyry begins by showing that animals are rational.[27] In a way this is true, but it is not necessary for Porphyry to start this way; he does so only because his opponents deny animals the capacity to receive justice because they are irrational. Although Porphyry denies that animals are irrational, it is by no means clear that we could not be just to them even if they were. In any event, two sorts of reason (*logos*) can be considered, even from a Stoic point of view (2): internal and external, the latter of which is exhibited by speech.

BP (vol. 2, pp. 128–29) note that Aristotle delineates three categories of "speech": (1) inarticulate noises and groans, e.g., the sounds of insects (*psophos*); (2) organized sounds, as in the chirping of birds (*phone*); and (3) language per se, organized by semantic rules (*dialectos*).[28] Porphyry does not distinguish carefully between (1) and (2), and at times wants to say that animals have (3). Why does he think this is the case?

When a Greek hears an Indian or a Scythian, he does not understand him any more than he would understand a crane; only a clangor of long and short syllables is heard, without significance (3). Having once learned the language this person speaks, we should wonder whether the organized sounds of animals, which obviously have some communicative function among animals themselves, indicate a reasoning ability. The ancients (of a golden age?) were said to have understood the speech of animals. Before the reader assumes this was a Dr. Doolittle fantasy, he should consider the extensive scientific research efforts today to understand the sounds of whales and many other animals. Skeptics will be bolstered by the realization that some in antiquity were also doubtful:

> An associate, also, of mine informed me that he once had a boy for a servant, who understood the meaning of all the sounds of birds, and who said that all of them were prophetic, and declarative of what would shortly happen. He added that he was deprived of this knowledge through his mother, who, fearing that he would be sent to the Emperor as a gift, poured urine into his ear when he was asleep. [3]

Omitting this story through the passion for incredulity, Porphyry points to other phenomena. The fact that animals understand each other's sounds is important to notice (4), as Lorenz and other ethologists have done. Some animals even imitate human speech (e.g., parrots); the fact that not all do so does not necessarily indicate their lack of rationality, for we do not think of ourselves as lacking rationality if we do not know all languages. What is noteworthy is not the communication that does not occur but that which does, most of which is not mnemonic "parrot talk." Animals often understand across species lines, e.g., when birds indicate distress to mammals, or when human beings learn about the movements of a hare from a barking dog. Cowherds and shepherds know the wants of their animals from their lowing and bleating (5).

For every example of our understanding the sounds of animals, there is an example of their clearly understanding us (6).

They not only hear a voice as if it were a mere sound, but they also grasp our meaning (15). Dogs, horses, and the like obey commands, and it certainly seems to be stretching the case a bit too far to suggest that these commands are learned and interpreted "instinctively" or "by nature" (*phusei*). Curiously enough, when human beings do the things some animals can do, we are more than willing, on the same evidence, to attribute dialectic or at least syllogistic reasoning to them. A meat-eating human being, therefore, is not just ignoring animals through indifference (6): "For how is it possible that he should not defame and calumniate animals, who has determined to cut them in pieces, as if they were stones?"

The evidence animals offer of external reason through speech leads Porphyry to conclude that their internal reasoning ability is different only in degree, not in kind, from that of human beings (7).[29] Animals certainly can sense and are intelligent. Following Plutarch, Porphyry notices that the fact that human beings are more intelligent does not deny animal intelligence— the fact that hawks fly higher than partridges does not mean that partridges cannot fly (8).[30] Further, to designate animals as "mad" only makes sense against a background of rationality (again, à la Plutarch, 7, 24).

Some will think that Porphyry has legislated animal rationality into existence here, but Porphyry could always make the same charge regarding those who so quickly dismiss animal intelligence and communication as not being rational. In any event, Porphyry also sees animals exhibiting prudence (*phroneseos*—9); that is, animals are capable of certain types of awareness through nature (or instinct). Yet other types are learned from other animals or from men through discipline (10), which is a necessary condition for prudence.[31] Porphyry realizes that to use quasi-moral terms regarding some animals indicates that animals may have vices, like envy. Anticipating Lorenz, Porphyry realizes that it is the gregarious character of animals that allows us to see them in the social context required by this quasi-moral discourse (11).[32] To call animals savage does for moral discourse what calling them mad does for discourse about rationality (12). If men were reduced to brutish behavior with respect to food, how much more savage would we become? War is an indication of the lengths to which human beings will go when desires are frustrated, and the warrior has often been called immoral, especially when he kills the innocent. On the other hand, benevolence is not unknown among animals or human beings (13).

But could all of this be irrelevant to the real issue? Even if animals do not have what can strictly be called language or rationality, or be described in moral terms, do they not deserve our respect? The key to modern philosophical vegetarianism, sentience, can operate as a heuristic which illuminates the heart of Porphyry's theory, which Porphyry (and Plutarch) may have been only dimly aware of as the heart of their theories (see Porphyry's use of the argument from marginal cases, treated in chapter 5).

For Porphyry (21), everything animated (empsychon) is adapted to be sensitive (aisthetikon) and imaginative (phantastikon). To kill animals painlessly is almost unheard of, but even to do this would still be to deprive them of those ends they are capable of attaining. Expectation, memory, design, preparation, fear, indignation, and the like force Porphyry once again to slip yet another end into an animal's purview: reason. Plutarch's presence is clear here (22), especially when Porphyry responds to those who say that animals "as it were" are afraid, hear, or live. Opponents to vegetarianism often use as a standard of reason a perfect reason that the beasts fail to meet; but so do human beings (23). A man is more rational than a dog, who is more rational than a sheep, etc.; but a tree cannot be rational at all, in that it lacks the necessary condition of sentience.

In short, because justice for Porphyry consists in not injuring anything, it must be extended as far as every animated nature— or else we would have to deny justice not only to animals but to many human beings. However, a crude utilitarian calculus of pleasure (contrast with Singer's more sophisticated utilitarianism) cannot preserve justice (26–27). The cosmic scope of justice is exhibited in the following quote which in a way transcends the peculiarly Neoplatonic slant of Porphyry's words:

> But if an assimilation to divinity is the end of life, an innoxious (i.e., innocent—*ablabes*) conduct toward all things will be in the most eminent degree preserved. As, therefore, he who is led by his passions is innoxious only towards his children and his wife, but despises and acts fraudulently towards other persons, since in consequence of the irrational part predominating in him, he is excited to, and astonished about mortal concerns; but he who is led by reason, preserves an innoxious conduct towards his fellow citizens, and still more so towards strangers, and towards all men, through having the irrational part in subjection, and is therefore more rational and divine than the former character; thus also, he who does not confine harmless conduct to men alone, but extends it to other animals, is more similar to divinity; and if it was possible to extend it even to plants, he would preserve this image in a still greater degree. As, however, this is not possible, we may in this respect lament, with the ancients.[33]

Vegetarianism, for Porphyry, is thus not the dessert of the Neoplatonic meal, but a part of the main course.

Book Four, like Book Two, is not of great interest to modern readers, as it deals with the relationship between Greek vegetarianism and other ancient cultures, like those of Greece in the golden age (1–2), Lacedaemonia under Lycurgus (3–5), Egypt (6–10), and the culture of the Jews (11–13). Relying on Josephus, Porphyry pays particular attention to the Essenes, whose description resembles that of the original Pythagorean sect: common ownership of goods, frugality, etc. Although not vegetarian, they were at least somewhat sober in their eating of meat.[34]

The point of these cultural histories is that there have been many examples of vegetarian practice in different times and places.[35] Porphyry's treatment of Indian vegetarianism (17–18) is of interest in that it gives some indication of how this ancient center of vegetarianism may have influenced (directly or indirectly) Greeks like Pythagoras and Plotinus. The Greeks called the wise men of India Gymnosophists, one division of which was the Brahmin class, who ate fruits, milk, and herbs. The fertility of the Ganges region makes India sound like a paradise, sustaining the belief that the golden age still existed in remote parts of the world. Another class of Gymnosophists, the Samanaeans, ate rice, bread, fruit, and herbs, making both classes vegetarian. Porphyry obviously feels a kinship for these men, who sound like Neoplatonists in that they willingly endure their present life so as to be liberated from their bodies later. In the next chapter, I will treat the end of this incomplete Book Four.

7 ARETE, RORTY, AND HARTSHORNE

PHILOSOPHERS tend to discriminate four types of moral action, although these discriminations are sometimes implicit: (1) Some actions are morally neutral, hence morally permissible. (2) Some actions are morally wrong, hence we ought not to perform them. (3) Some actions are duties we ought to perform. And (4) some actions are above and beyond the call of duty, thus are morally permissible, but are not morally neutral; these praiseworthy actions are called supererogatory.[1] What sort of action is vegetarianism?

All will agree that vegetarianism is not morally wrong, so we are left with alternatives (1), (3), and (4). To say that choosing a vegetarian diet over a meat-eating diet is a morally neutral decision, like choosing to eat with a fork or a spoon, is to beg the question as to whether animals deserve our respect. In fact, those who try to justify or allow meat-eating often do so on *moral* grounds, either implicitly or explicitly (e.g., Hermarchus or Claudius the Neopolitan). The enormous attention recently paid to philosophical vegetarianism indicates that not even most antivegetarians perceive it as morally neutral. To do so is to trivialize it.

We are left with the question, Is vegetarianism (3) or (4)? One might suspect that the status of philosophical vegetarianism would be more exalted if it were supererogatory. But if it is a practice above and beyond the call of duty it would not necessarily have any implications for those of us who are mere mortals. If one assumes that one is not duty-bound to abstain from animal flesh, then philosophical vegetarianism would indeed appear supererogatory. Inasmuch as most philosophers from the end of the classical period until rather recently have made this assumption, it is not surprising that the vegetarian is popularly perceived as having gone beyond the call of duty in his dietary regimen. Yet as a famous American vegetarian, Thoreau, once put it, there are continents and seas in the moral world yet unexplored, and each person is an isthmus to that world. But, "How worn and dusty, then, must be the highways of the world, how deep the ruts of tradition and conformity!"[2]

My readers should not get the impression that contemporary philosophers are flocking to vegetarianism. Rather, the debate regarding philosophical vegetarianism has been heated. Nonetheless, the mode of argument used by contemporary philosophical vegetarians is a standard one. It does not begin with a definition of ethical concepts and high-level pronouncements. The method is to

> identify what seem to be the major outlines of our *considered* moral beliefs, and then to bring logical analysis to bear on these to see whether they square with our apparent *unconsidered* attitude toward the particular matter under investigation. [My emphasis][3]

In the case of our treatment of animals, the contemporary philosophical vegetarian holds that our considered moral belief (or moral truism, as Nielson puts it[4]) that unnecessary suffering should be avoided does *not* square with our unconsidered eating of animal flesh, leading many meat-eating philosophers into a highly casuistical "anthropodicy," a term Clark invents to parallel the theist's problem with theodicy.[5]

The approach of Greek philosophical vegetarians was slightly different. They were not so much concerned with "considered moral beliefs" as with excellence (*arete*), or with what some Romans would call the ideal of *humanitas*. It is this striving to become the best human being one can become that differentiates Greek vegetarianism from its contemporary counterpart, not the primitive belief in transmigration or the like, whose importance has been overemphasized by several commentators.

An *arete*-based approach to vegetarianism is not necessarily supererogatory. Six possible states of moral character can be imagined, which may help us locate what sort of action vegetarianism is, with the most moral character at the top:[6]

A. Heroic excellence (*arete*): when one wants to act well, and does so heroically.

    H1: nonsupererogatory heroism.

    H2: supererogatory heroism.

B. Ordinary excellence (*arete*): when one wants to act well, and does so.

C. Self-control (*enkrateia*): when one wants to act badly, but controls oneself.

D. Lack of self-control (*akrasia*): when one wants to act badly, tries to control oneself, but cannot.

E. Badness of character (*kakia*): when one wants to act badly, does so without resistance, thinking it to be good.

F. Brutishness (*aischros*): a diseased moral character, inhuman.

"To act well" with respect to animals means—at the very least, if Plutarch and Porphyry are right—avoiding unnecessary suffering or killing. In civilized society where vegetal food is abundant, this means that to attain (B) or (C) one *must* be a vegetarian. This in turn means that opponents to vegetarianism exhibit moral characters (D), (E), or in extreme cases of animal torture, (F). Moral character (D) is more prevalent than many suspect. Philosophical vegetarians often hear their colleagues admit that the vegetarian's case is probably right (thereby indicating that vegetarianism is not a morally neutral practice), but nonetheless jokingly talk about cows or pigs as they eat their roast beef or ham sandwiches. Nervous laughter usually follows. The existence of moral character (E) probably indicates that there are some basic disagreements about the moral status of animals, the status of rights claims, or some other issue. I hope that a consideration of the ancient vegetarians can clear up at least some of these disagreements.

If Plutarch, Porphyry, et al., are right in implying that the attainment of (B) or (C) would require dutiful vegetarianism, then of what would heroic excellence (A) consist? Two sorts of heroism could be imagined.[7] One could be a heroic vegetarian if he did his duty—not causing animals to suffer or be killed unnecessarily—regularly under conditions in which desire or self-interest or some other reason would prod most people not to do it, even though vegetal food was in abundance—H1. Or one could be a heroic vegetarian by refusing, above and beyond the call of duty, to make animals suffer or be killed even if it might be deemed "necessary" as in times of drought, etc.—H2. That is, moral excellence in the form of (B) or (A) can be attained without supererogation, although (A) can also be supererogatory, as in H2. Another example of a nonsupererogatory heroism would be the case of a doctor who stayed by his patients in a plague-ridden city when all of his fellow doctors fled; and supererogation can also be seen in the case of a doctor who *volunteered* to go to a plague-ridden city. If the first doctor were interviewed after the plague he might well say, "I only did my (Hippocratic) duty." But only a modesty so excessive as to appear false could make the second doctor say the same. So also, vegetarians in a predominantly meat-eating and affluent culture may be nonsupererogatory heroes merely by doing their duty. To quote Urmson:

> While life in a world without its saints and heroes would be impoverished, it would only be poor and not necessarily brutish or short as when basic duties are neglected. If we are to exact basic duties like debts, and censure failure,

such duties must be, in ordinary circumstances, within the capacity of the ordinary man. . . . A line must be drawn between what we can expect and demand from others and what we can merely hope for and receive with gratitude when we get it.[8]

Note that from the perspective of animals raised for the table, life *is* brutish and short. The key question seems to be, Is vegetarianism "within the capacity of the ordinary man"? If not, Plutarch's and Porphyry's claim that it is a duty would be in danger, for vegetarianism would slip into the category of supererogation, thereby rendering it largely irrelevant for those who are not moral heroes in the sense of H2.

Porphyry himself admits in *De abstinentia* (IV, 8) that the law grants to the general population many things which cannot be granted to the philosopher. They can legitimately associate with prostitutes or spend all of their free time in a tavern; today we would say that it is their right as free agents to do these things. But the legitimacy of civil liberties in the political arena is not always an accurate guide regarding questions of what we ought to do in the moral arena. Porphyry's claim that those things which are permitted to the multitude cannot be permitted to the philosopher is not a defense of the supposed sagelike, disembodied character of thought in the Hellenistic era; rather, it is an affirmation of the primacy of reason in the philosopher's life. Regan comes close to Porphyry's point here when he holds that it is not irredeemably wrong (for the multitude?) to eat meat, but most of those (philosophers?) who read his essay are meat eaters who ought to change.[9] Or, as Porphyry has it (IV, 20):

As water which flows through a rock is more uncorrupted than that which runs through marshes, because it does not bring with it much mud; thus, also, the soul which administers its own affairs in a body that is dry, and is not moistened by the juices of foreign flesh, is in a more excellent condition, is more uncorrupted.

Both Porphyry and Regan (perhaps also Plutarch) imply that vegetarianism is a duty for philosophers, but supererogatory for the multitude. The problem with this dichotomy is not that it expects too much from the philosopher, but that it expects too little from the multitude. In our egalitarian, or somewhat egalitarian, culture why is it not possible to encourage *all* human beings to pursue *arete*? Both Porphyry and Regan could have benefited from the distinctions I have made above. Perhaps what they are trying to discern could be stated more accurately as follows: vegetarianism is a duty (see the arguments from sentiency and marginal cases). In the present state of culture, however, and this applies to Porphyry as well, a certain heroism is required from philosophers, but especially from the multitude, in order to meet this duty. This heroism need not be supererogatory; that is, one only needs H1 to fulfill one's duty.

To defend vegetarianism as a duty, it is not necessary to argue that animals have "natural" rights. Neither Regan nor Singer builds his case on such rights, but both can still object to meat-eating because it causes nontrivial pain, usually by denying equal, if any, consideration to pain whenever it is inflicted on an animal.[10] One of the advantages of Greek thought is that it could easily consider the issue of animal suffering without raising the issue of necessary and sufficient conditions for rights at all. As Steinbock shows, it is wrong to punch someone because it infringes on his rights, but we could also say it is wrong because it hurts him. This reason would extend not only to human beings but also to all sentient creatures, even if they did not possess rights.[11] Although suffering, mattering, valuing, taking an interest in, caring, and the like may have subtly varied peculiarities, they are roughly synonymous and are opposed to a state of indifference to the experiences of animals.[12]

Perhaps the strongest argument against vegetarianism, whether ancient or modern, is that we can avoid animal suffering by killing them painlessly. But as Singer notices:

Practically and psychologically it is impossible to be consistent in one's concern for nonhuman animals while continuing to dine on them. If we are prepared to take the life of another being merely in order to satisfy our taste for a particular type of food, then that being is no more than a means to our end. In time we will come to regard pigs, cattle, and chickens as things for us to use, no matter how strong our compassion may be.[13]

This time had come as early as the days of the Stoics. And in practical terms it is impossible to rear animals for food on a large scale without inflicting suffering. Even animals slaughtered on the most "idyllic" farms or in the wild are just as dead as the animals slaughtered on ruthless modern farms.[14] Animals have an interest in living, as is indicated both by their ardent efforts to avoid forces capable of killing them and by their communications to us when such forces are met. Cows have managed to let us know that they do not want to die. How does sneaking up on a cow to kill it make any difference in principle? It certainly does seem strange that inflicting pain on an animal is a "hurt," but killing it is legitimate.[15]

Even stranger is the suggestion that a person has something to live for only if he can formulate long-range plans about the future, and if he has the rationality to carry out those plans.[16] Does this mean that there is no reason for "marginal cases" (or the happy-go-lucky) to be kept alive? Or that Socrates' death, quite apart from his belief in immortality, should not be regretted because he was seventy years old anyway? Fox also misses the point when he assumes that the vegetarian is suggesting that capacity for suffering is a universal characteristic of beings that are worthy of consideration.[17] What of those, he asks, who have that congenital disease where there is indifference to pain? The vegetarian, however, does not have to hold that sentience is a necessary condition for moral consideration; rather, the capacity to suffer is sufficient for a being to be worthy of moral consideration. To claim to be opposed to animal cruelty and yet eat meat is to deserve the irony of the eighteenth-century humanitarian, Oliver Goldsmith: "They pity, and they eat the objects of their compassion."[18]

The plausibility of the philosophical vegetarian's claims, particularly those of the ancient philosophical vegetarians, becomes apparent when one considers Richard Rorty's book *Philosophy and the Mirror of Nature*, one of the most important philosophical works in the last decade. In a chapter entitled "Pre-Linguistic Awareness," Rorty holds that we ought to abandon the "Platonic urge" to ground our moral prohibitions on an ontology of nature (pp. 182–92). This claim is important in its own right and as an instance of Rorty's defense of hermeneutics. Apparently, Rorty's discussion is not so much intended to be a justification of a position as a diagnosis of how we think about and deal with prelinguistic beings, especially nonhuman animals. But eventually this diagnosis reaches a conclusion which needs justification, that "we send pigs to slaughter with equanimity . . . [and] this is not 'irrational'" (p. 190). I claim that Rorty's treatment of nonhuman animals is not sufficient to establish the case for meat-eating, as Rorty seems to think. Although Rorty never treats meat-eating explicitly, I assume that pigs are sent to slaughter mainly to be eaten.

In an analysis of Sellars, Rorty admits that some nonhuman beings (e.g., rats, amoebas, computers) are capable of awareness, and some human beings without language can experience pain, e.g., infants (pp. 182–83). But although language does not change the quality of our experience, it does let us enter a community whose members can exchange justifications of assertions (p. 185). This is not a community of feeling, but a linguistic community in which rights are dependent on a person's relations with others to whom (or to which) he can speak (p. 187). That is, moral prohibitions against hurting others, the nature of a moral community, and the grounds for ascribing rights are not dependent on facts of nature, like sentience; to believe in a community of feeling as the basis for moral prohibitions is to fall victim to the dreaded "Platonic urge" (p. 191). Rather, moral prohibitions and rights are attributed on the basis of a being's membership in a linguistic community.

For Rorty, the nonconceptual, nonlinguistic knowledge of a raw feel (e.g., pain) is attributed on the basis of a being's potential membership in the social practice of a linguistic community (pp. 188–89). "Babies and the more attractive sorts of animal," like bats (?) and koala bears, are credited with "having feelings," whereas photoelectric cells, pigs, spiders, and amoebas are not so credited. In Rorty's linguistic sense, this community feeling unites us with anything humanoid. To be humanoid "is to have a human face, and the most important part of that face is a mouth which we can imagine uttering sentences." That is, we can imagine babies opening their mouths and speaking about the presence of pain, but we cannot imagine spiders or pigs doing so.

The point Rorty wants to make is that moral prohibitions against hurting babies are not "ontologically grounded" in their possession of feeling (p. 190). In fact, it is the other way around. We do not move, as the ancient philosophers supposed, from an awareness of feelings in others to moral prohibitions designed to protect these others, but rather from moral prohibitions to an attribution of feeling: "The moral prohibitions are expressions of a sense of community based on the imagined possibility of conversation, and the attribution of feelings is little more than a reminder of these prohibitions" (p. 190). Rorty's account seems to be that:

1. If X is an actual or potential member of a linguistic community, or if we attribute language to X, then it is wrong to hurt X.
2. If it is wrong to hurt X, then X is an actual or potential member of a community of feeling, or we attribute feelings to X.
3. To attribute feelings to X is only to remind ourselves that it is wrong to hurt X.

Because Rorty is as important a philosopher as there is in America today, he merits attention, no matter how implausible some of his accounts are. The following five points should be sufficient to cast doubt on his view of pigs and to support my claim.

1. The first difficulty with Rorty's account arises when he ad-

mits that pigs do much better on intelligence tests than koalas (p. 190). Why, then, do we attribute feelings to koalas but not to pigs? [19] Because "pigs don't writhe in quite the right humanoid way, and the pig's face is the wrong shape for the facial expressions which go with ordinary conversation" (p. 190). One suspects that the "attractive" humanoid features of koalas are arbitrary grounds for attributing feelings to them but not to pigs. I for one—and I am not alone—do not find koalas (or bats!) more "attractive" than pigs; nor can I more easily imagine them speaking than pigs. [20] Rorty's description of the way in which "we" care about koalas but not pigs amounts to a factual empirical claim that is not universally true.

2. One wonders how Rorty can legitimately say that pigs "writhe." If to writhe means, as the OED suggests, "a twinge of *pain*" or "to contort the body, limbs, etc., as from *agony, emotion*" (my emphasis), then how can Rorty say pigs writhe? Inasmuch as they lack attractive humanoid features, or mouths that we can imagine speaking, we should not, on Rorty's account, be able to attribute pain, agony, or emotion to them.

3. Rorty may try to escape objection (2) by appealing to his two different senses of awareness. Awareness-1 is manifested by rats, amoebas, computers, and presumably pigs, and consists merely in "reliable signaling" (p. 182). Awareness-2 is

> manifested only by beings whose behavior we construe as the utterance of sentences with the intention of justifying the utterance of other sentences. In this latter sense awareness is justified true belief—knowledge—but in the former sense it is the ability to respond to stimuli. [Pp. 182–83]

If Rorty is suggesting that a pig's writhing is only awareness-1, then his attribution of feelings to koalas, bats, and babies (not pigs) must mean that koalas, bats, and babies are capable of, or we can imagine them capable of, awareness-2. Once again, this seems arbitrary, especially when one notices Rorty's use of the term "behavior" in the above quote. As far as I know, koalas and bats exhibit no behavior that pigs do not exhibit that can be construed "as the utterance of sentences with the intention of justifying the utterance of other sentences." Nor is it clear that infants exhibit such behavior. Therefore, Rorty's imagined possibility of conversation with bats and koala bears would be based *solely* on the shape of their mouths. Further, to lump rats and pigs, on the one hand, together with amoebas and computers, on the other, is misleading. One finds it difficult, if not impossible, to imagine what it would mean to say that a computer writhed, and hence had experienced pain, agony, or emotion. Yet it is so easy to say that a pig can writhe that even Rorty says so.

4. I have twice accused Rorty of arbitrariness, to which he might respond that the charge is irrelevant in that *any* distinction regarding who should have rights is somewhat arbitrary. The case of animals is similar, he might say, to his example of adult rights granted to a person on his eighteenth birthday (p. 187). There is nothing clear-cut about this date, but after the eighteenth birthday there *is* a shift in the way a person relates to others. Line-drawing may be "injudicious," but it is neither a mistake nor irrational. What might be unfair, for Rorty, would be to grant adult rights to all eighteen year olds, except for some chosen people, who would have to wait until they were thirty. He might analogously argue that it would be fair, though arbitrary, to slaughter pigs, but unfair to make exceptions for some pigs.

This stance is troublesome for several reasons. Whereas one's eighteenth birthday is an arbitrary date for acquiring adult rights—because there is no precise time at which people, in general, become suited for the possession of such rights—it is *not* arbitrary to say that most people should not be given them at age five and should already have been given them by age forty. There is no reason to pick the day a person becomes eighteen rather than the day before or the day after his birthday, but any of the three would obviously be far better than the fifth birthday or the fortieth birthday. So, too, do shrimp and oysters, as Singer notices, fall into a grey area concerning our decision as to whether they experience pain; and if they do feel pain, whether it is wrong to hurt them.[21] But pigs do not occupy such a grey area, as Rorty unwittingly admits when he notices them writhing.

5. To send a pig to slaughter involves a decision, which Rorty not only makes, but makes in the case of pigs with "equanimity." This might imply only that the person who sends pigs to slaughter is calm and composed, and is not irrational. The word equanimity, however, as defined by the OED, carries with it the notion of "*fairness* of judgement, impartiality, *equity*" (my emphasis), which indicates anything but arbitrariness, in that fairness and equity are, by definition, opposed to arbitrariness. If it is *fair* to slaughter a pig, or a matter of *equity*, then Rorty must do two things. First, he must avoid the charge of arbitrariness, and not just in the minimal sense of slaughtering some pigs but making exceptions for others; i.e., he must find a nonarbitrary basis for slaughtering pigs at all. And second, he must at the same time avoid the "Platonic urge" to make his position nonarbitrary by appealing to some fact of nature. It is hard to see how Rorty can accomplish either one of these tasks, much less both. Or, he might try to avoid objection (5) altogether by refraining from the use of the term "equanimity."

Although I will not offer an adequate alternative to Rorty's account of prelinguistic awareness in pigs, I can suggest how one might surrender to the "Platonic urge" without building moral prohibitions on "old style" metaphysics. The fact that Rorty noticed pigs writhing indicates that pigs *do* communicate in their own way. Although Rorty may be right, along with Hegel (p. 192)—that the individual human being apart from society (and especially, for Rorty, its linguistic conventions) "is just one more animal"—it does not follow that it is legitimate to inflict unnecessary suffering on "just one more animal." Pigs and other animals indicate to us through writhing that they are capable not only of awareness-1—even if they fall short of awareness-2—but also of experiencing pain, as Rorty might have to reluctantly admit. It is just not true that human language is the only (or at times, the most reliable) guide to the feelings, interests, or pains of other beings. In the case of human beings, language can *disguise* facts as well as communicate them. If a dog's whimpering and clawing at the door cannot inform one of the animal's need to go out, then neither can the student's verbal and plaintive request that he has to go to the bathroom. In fact, the student may be lying. Rorty seems to have fallen victim to the dogma that there is a vast gulf between natural and conventional (humanoid) bearers of meaning, giving rise to the gulf between the ways we treat nonhumanoid animals and men. At best this gulf is a difference in degree.[22] Perhaps he should consider that many, if not most, of the attributions of pain we grant to other human beings are based not on articulated evidence, but on writhings, moans, the sight of blood, and so on, all of which are exhibited by pigs. In the meantime, it seems that Rorty has not so much destroyed as clouded the mirror of nature. It is to Rorty's credit, however, that he is one of the few to notice that to give in to the "Platonic urge" is to endanger our equanimity when we slaughter pigs, as I suggested in chapter 4.

What is amazing is the plurality of ontologies and ethics which can support the case for vegetarianism, in that it needs only the suffering of animals as a starting point. This is why Neoplatonists, Peripatetics, utilitarians, analytic philosophers, process philosophers, and phenomenologists can all argue for vegetarianism. The only significant factor that seems to be missing from ancient thought is the idea of a radically one-directional theory of evolution through time.[23] Something like an "appetite" for value or "mental pole" runs all the way through nature, with the ultimate material units of process themselves acting as processes. This new discovery of continuity in nature, both from a physical and biological point of view, is in a way a rediscovery of the Greek realization that human beings *are* able to recognize the feelings of other animals, contra Rorty. As Brumbaugh states: "We seem to have followed a long circuit and come back to the world of the ancient Greeks, a world of nature alive—but we have come back with a new sense of individual human dignity and ethical compassion."[24]

Perhaps the most sophisticated version of this rediscovery and reworking of certain Greek themes (rather than a rejection of them, as in Rorty) is found in the recent thought of Charles

Hartshorne.[25] Hartshorne is among that minority of philosophers who are panpsychists, or as he calls them, psychicalists.
He holds that anything concrete feels, omitting from the picture
abstractions like "blue," and collections of concrete individuals
like "two cats," which may feel individually, but not collec-
tively (CS, 141). Of course tables do not feel, but that does not
mean that there is no feeling *in* them. Although the table is
"relatively concrete," it is really a collection of more concrete
singulars: molecules, or better, atoms. As contemporary physics
has made apparent, these concrete singulars *do* shows signs of
spontaneous activity and sensitivity to the environment around
them. "Mere matter," construed as "the zero of feeling," is an
absolute negation whose meaning is wholly parasitic on what it
denies (CS, 143). Nothing has ever been observed which logically could not exist with experience; even inert rocks have ac-
tive atoms, molecules or particles (CS, 160–61). Hartshorne
holds, along with Leibniz, that no positive meaning can be
given to the negative of "sentient," because all concrete things
react to their environments (CS, 35, 112–13). If all concrete individuals are sentient, does "sentient individual" lose its distinctive meaning? Not necessarily, because as in the case of the
table, many pseudo-individual entities are not sentient individuals at all. Trees, for example, are essentially collectives, colo-
nies of cells without any unity comparable either to that of
single cells or to that which a nervous system gives vertebrates
(CS, 142).

Nature is in some sense a single enterprise, and inasmuch as
ethics is concerned with social relations, it is not irrelevant to
view our very bodies as instances of social relations among
cells. As Hartshorne puts it, "If our cells were not uncon-
sciously, instinctively ethical . . . we could not be consciously
so" (FH, 154). A tree (or a plant) is many things taken as one,
but it is not really in a deep sense one. Lacking a nervous system, its many cells are, for the most part, "on their own."
Hartshorne quotes Aristotle here to good effect: "A tree is like a
sleeping man who never wakes up" (FH, 155). A "higher" animal, at least, is in addition an individual when taken as a

whole; because it has a nervous system its many cells are not on their own, but are part of a psychological (not just physiological) unity. Thus, two levels of sentient experience are found in animals: (1) the experiences of each concrete individual at a microscopic level, which occur in plants and rocks as well—S1; and (2) sentiency per se, which consists in those experiences, lapsing in dreamless sleep, that enable the animal as a whole to feel pain, or at times to remember or anticipate pain, i.e., to suffer (FH, 156)—S2. Because S1 is sufficient to refute the materialist, but not sufficient to attribute pain or suffering to plants— where S2 is needed—plants can be eaten with equanimity, even if they too have some inherent value (whatever that means in this context) because of S1. "To cut down a tree is not analogous to killing a deer or even a fish, but rather to destroying a colony of paramecia or bacteria" (FH, 155). We object to pain in animals, however, because it is they who suffer, and not simply their cells. In the case of human beings, as well, the most direct contact with physical reality is what happens inside our body, particularly in our nervous systems, when cellular feeling occurs; only then do we feel. Thus, if we really know ourselves, we know a great deal about animals, and in a peculiar way a great deal about the rest of nature by way of contrast (DW, 82, 85).

Human beings are animals, too. One of the important differences between human beings and the other higher animals, including those that are eaten, is the symbolic capacity of human beings, shown primarily in language (FH, 160–62):

> The greater our power to generalize, the greater range of options we can entertain for carrying out our purposes. . . . A fox may have the options of chasing a rabbit and searching for field mice. But without a system of symbols this power is narrowly limited. A man can go on a hunger strike, or become a vegetarian, or cease being a vegetarian.

The reality of genuinely open possibilities does not have to imply, as Rorty thinks, that values are wholly determined by the way we speak, but may suggest why life is tragic (FH, 164). Because human beings are self-conscious participants in the cosmic drama, they are trustees for a cosmic end, as opposed to tyrants over all else. But there is a price for humanity's superior reason, compassion, and language. Lesser creatures—who are "lesser" not because of their sentience (S2) if they are animals—are "infallible servants of the cosmic cause" (FH, 169). Human beings, however, can reject their duties or refuse to be compassionate (FH, 170). Animals do their best: they care for their young; they try to help their mates and, in some species, their fellows; and in some cases they even care for those outside of their species. Human beings must *choose* to attain *arete*.

If infants have actual rights, and Hartshorne thinks they do, then so do the higher animals, whose sentient experiences are on a much higher level (FH, 167). Yet Hartshorne's adherence to the argument from marginal cases is not meant to belittle human nature. Dogs think "doggishly," but for all we know, a dog cannot think that he is thinking doggishly. Human beings are equally imprisoned by their own nature, but they know that this is so. "To know a mental limit as such is to be, in some sense and degree, beyond that limit" (CM, 208). Because of this power of generalization it is easy for human beings to suppose that they can escape *all* anthropomorphic limitations, but this is not the case.

Human beings can only partially transcend their animality, yet they often tragically abuse their partial superiority, as Hartshorne states in this Porphyry-like passage:

> Man is the animal that surveys the animal kingdom and his own place in that kingdom, that surveys the vegetable and mineral realms and the place of animals in the general pattern of nature. More than that, man is the animal that sees the entire world as an arbitrary instance possible kinds of world. [CM, 208]

It is perhaps such a belief in the arbitrariness of the world which allows Rorty and others, but not Hartshorne, to send pigs to slaughter with equanimity. Animals have rights, for Hartshorne. Or if the word "rights" is bothersome, they have, in Regan-like fashion, "intrinsic value" (FH, 170). Value, for Hartshorne, is not the absolute Kant takes it to be. If animals lack an absolute quality of rationality, then Hartshorne would call our attention to the fact that human beings also lack this quality, as Kantians would reluctantly have to admit. From this point of view no animal, not even a human being, is an end in himself; only God is. As in the case of Theophrastus's relationship with Aristotle, Hartshorne tries to show that on Kant's own grounds he should have had a different view of animals. Kant says that only a rational will that acts according to its rationality is intrinsically or unqualifiedly good; human beings so act only imperfectly or incompletely; only God always and entirely conforms to rational requirements (RS, 50).[26] Therefore, Kant's position should have been either that all animals, even human beings, are dispensable, or that the contribution of somewhat rational human animals to the *Summum Bonum* is not absolutely different—as Kant thinks—from the contribution of animals of lesser, or perhaps even nonexistent, rationality. Terrestrial, nonhuman life is not the final end of all existence, but neither is human life, according to Hartshorne, Kant, and the Neoplatonists. This fact should help us realize that the "significant analogy between a dog in pain and a man in pain" means that we should "prevent or mitigate animal pain whenever it occurs or threatens" (FH, 171).

Our relationship to the nonhuman world, for Hartshorne, is one of a

> cautiously positive form of anthropomorphism—that which attributes to other creatures neither the duplication, nor the total absence, but lesser degrees and more primitive forms, of those properties exhibited in high degree, and more refined or complex forms, of those in us. [RS, 52]

If we ask whether a plant's parts possess adaptability, creativity, or sentience, we would have to say, very little. "But the difference between zero and a finite positive quantity makes *all* the difference when we are seeking the general principles of reality" (RS, 52).

Where there is feeling there is valuing or mattering, and in more than an instrumental sense.[27] But we need not give up the common-sense view that vegetables and rivers are insentient. Low intensity of feeling cannot be tragic, but the high intensity of feeling in animals (S2) makes them candidates for a tragic end (RS, 54–55): "The morally good individual is one who wills to *optimize* the harmony and intensity of living for all those lives he or she is in a position to affect" (my emphasis—RS, 55). The search for *arete* would include vegetarianism—even if there were no rigid distinction between plants and animals—because of the *degree* of feeling that can be optimized in the latter.

We can, and should, consider "nourishing ourselves more largely by direct use of vegetable food, rather than by the very wasteful method of giving this food to animals whose flesh we ultimately eat" (RS, 58). Complete vegetarianism is probably not the most appropriate solution to this problem of developing an efficient and equitable distribution of the earth's food resources for human beings, even if it is the most appropriate solution, or the first step in that direction, to fair treatment of animals. Hartshorne, like Ovid (see chapter 2), calls our attention to the fact that vegetarianism is only one (albeit important) part of an overall need to respect our ecosystem, which would include preservation of soil, water, natural grasses, and minerals. Another part would be to make sure that our pets' diets did not depend on the slaughter of whales or other animals, as is now the case. Artificially overpopulated and maintained species (i.e., pet species and those that are eaten) also need to have limited reproduction if they are not to offend the inclusive ecosystem, i.e., if they are not to contribute unwittingly to hunger in others.

Ironically, we are now at a stage of technological development when all in the world should be well nourished, yet technology has intensified the desire to eat meat. Witness the incredible yields of millions of acres of corn in the Midwest—to feed equally incredible numbers of animals raised for the table. Something worse than mere bad taste is involved in a meat-eating diet (EC, 104): animals suffer unnecessarily, and they are killed unnecessarily, food is grown inefficiently while human beings starve, and future generations are ignored by today's wasteful land uses. Our most inclusive obligation, for Hartshorne, is to optimize our gifts to the future, including our gift of present happiness. Sentient life encompasses more than just human life. But in Neoplatonic fashion Hartshorne has spent a career arguing that even sentient life symbolizes rather than constitutes the Encompassing,

> the other animals live largely by feeling; we have to live far more by thought. Merely practical or scientific thinking only makes us extremely clever animals. Religious or philosophical thought alone can lift our feelings to the full human level on which we dare to face not simply this bit or that bit of the future but the future as such. [EC, 106–7]

Those unconvinced by the ancient vegetarians' arguments will probably not be convinced by Hartshorne; yet his defense of Wordsworth's view of nature indicates that he is not uncomfortable with the label "romanticist," which is not a synonym for "crazy metaphysics," as Macaulay thought (DW, 80).

Animals have feelings, but more important, they have feelings *of* cellular feelings. To refuse to generalize feeling as the stuff of nature, particularly animal nature, is to condemn our knowledge to the extremely abstract sort that is similar to the abstractions which allowed Descartes to view animals as he did (DW, 85). We are all contributors to a cosmic future; "With proper humility we may be able to cease flattering ourselves with the fancy that we or our species is the Everlasting." We may be of more value than many sparrows (FH, 171–72). But only by refusing to make absolute our difference from the rest of the animal world can we more easily open our minds to the really significant difference between *any* animal and the Everlasting.

NOTES

1 Introduction

1. Peter Singer, *Animal Liberation* (New York: New York Review, 1975), pp. 202–34.
2. Michael Fox, "Animal Liberation: A Critique," *Ethics* 88 (January 1978): 106.
3. I have no idea what Haussleiter ate; I am only suggesting that there is no indication in his work that philosophical vegetarianism is a contemporary issue.
4. A study of Eastern vegetarianism would surely be worthwhile, but it is beyond the bounds of the narrowly circumscribed philosophical treatment I intend. This contraction of vision will also force me to largely neglect varieties of vegetarianism in Greek culture that are more obviously due to myth or religion.
5. It has often been noticed that the Old Testament, despite characters such as Deborah, is a sexist document. What is little noticed is that it is equally unfair to animals; a woman and an animal are responsible for the Fall. For similar remarks on the Old Testament see Peter Singer, *Animal Liberation*, pp. 204–5. I owe a great debt to Singer's chapter "Man's Dominion," pp. 202–34, for the development of chapter 1. Also of service is John Passmore, "The Treatment of Animals," *Journal of the History of Ideas* (April–May 1975): 195–218.
6. Singer, *Animal Liberation*, pp. 209, 210. See St. Augustine, *The Catholic and Manichean Ways of Life*, trans. D. A. Gallagher and L. J. Gallagher (Boston: Catholic University Press, 1966), p. 102. Also see John Passmore, *Man's Responsibility for Nature* (New York: Scribner's, 1974), p. 111.

7. See Passmore, "Treatment of Animals," p. 196. The intricate communion symbolism suggests that Christ's body and blood are ingested just as much as the kid's. It should be noted that in the early centuries of the church, Christians were often criticized for the primitiveness of their sacred meal. A general treatment of the relationship between Christianity and animals can be found in C. W. Hume, *The Status of Animals in the Christian Religion* (London, 1956).

8. Passmore, "Treatment of Animals," p. 197; St. Augustine, *The Catholic and Manichean Ways of Life*, p. 91; St. Augustine, *City of God*, I, 20. Also see Philip E. Devine, "The Moral Basis of Vegetarianism," *Philosophy* 53 (1978): 504.

9. Homily XXIX, 471 in *Homilies of St. John Chrysostom on the Epistle of St. Paul to the Romans* (Oxford, 1861).

10. See Passmore, "Treatment of Animals," pp. 198, 199. The prayer goes as follows: "And for these also, O Lord, the humble beasts who bear with us the heat and burden of the day, we beg thee to extend thy great kindness of heart, for thou hast promised to save both man and beast, and great is thy loving-kindness, O Master." Paradoxically, St. Basil may be relying on St. Paul. See Romans 8:19–22.

11. See a delightful story in the preface to Singer's *Animal Liberation* about an "animal lover" chewing on a ham sandwich.

12. Ibid., pp. 215–16. See *St. Francis of Assisi, His Life and Writings as Recorded by His Contemporaries*, trans. L. Sherley-Price (London, 1959), p. 145. On the nature of fasting and abstinence (mostly from meat) in the history of Christianity, see Rudolph Arbesmann, "Fasting and Prophecy in Pagan and Christian Antiquity," *Traditio* 7 (1949): 1–71. For my purposes it needs only to be said that the reasons for fasting and meat abstinence have nothing to do with concern for animals, but with other concerns: asceticism, imitation of biblical practices, etc.

13. Dominican Fathers, trans., Third Book, pt. II, chap. CXII.

14. I apologize for calling nonhuman animals just "animals" throughout this book. It can be a misleading designation. See Mary Midgley, "The Concept of Beastliness," *Philosophy* 48 (1973): 111–35.

15. See Devine, "Moral Basis of Vegetarianism," pp. 502–3.

16. See Singer, *Animal Liberation*, pp. 9, 27 passim.

17. *Summa Theologiae*, IIa IIae, question 64, art. 1.

18. Ibid., question 65, art. 3.

19. This point was not lost on Hamlet, who alludes to this piece of scripture; see Act V, Scene 2. Indirectly I am respectfully implying an inconsistency on the part of Jesus, who was no vegetarian.

20. Anthony J. Povilitis, "On Assigning Rights to Animals and Nature," *Environmental Ethics* 2 (1980): 68.

21. Stephen R. L. Clark, *The Moral Status of Animals* (Oxford: Clarendon

Press, 1977), pp. 110, 191. Also see Andrew Linzey, *Animal Rights: A Christian Assessment of Man's Treatment of Animals* (London: SCM Press, 1976).

22. See Singer, *Animal Liberation*, pp. 213–14. Also Passmore, "The Treatment of Animals," p. 203. I am tempted here to reemphasize the links among racism-sexism-speciesism. That St. Thomas was a sexist there can be no doubt; but it is also interesting to notice that in the attempt to show that men must be compassionate he suggests, in a patronizing way, that Jews are particularly given to cruelty. His attitude toward the Moslem is even more well known. Again, see Passmore, p. 201.

23. See Singer, *Animal Liberation*, pp. 216–17, on the Renaissance. Also see Pico della Mirandola, *Oration on the Dignity of Man*; E. McCurdy, *The Mind of Leonardo da Vinci* (London: Cape, 1932), p. 78; Montaigne, "Apology for Raimond de Sebonde," in *The Works of Michel de Montaigne*, trans. William Hazlitt (1865).

24. Descartes, *Discourse on Method* in *Philosophical Works of Descartes*, trans. E. S. Haldane and G. R. T. Ross (London: Cambridge University Press), vol. I, pp. 115–18.

25. See Gareth B. Matthews, "Animals and the Unity of Psychology," *Philosophy* 53 (1978): 437–54.

26. Descartes's position would be even more flawed when chimps with sign language are considered.

27. See Leonora Rosenfield, *From Beast-Machine to Man-Machine* (New York: Octagon Books, 1968), p. 54. This fine book, originally published by Oxford University Press in 1940, deals with animal soul in French thought from Descartes's beast-machine, to the Aristotelian and Neoplatonic anti-Cartesians, to the empiricists, some of whom considered themselves Epicureans. See p. 73: "No unified anti-Cartesian movement regarding animal nature existed," yet two main sorts of attack developed. First, adherents to older theological traditions criticized Descartes from an Aristotelian point of view regarding his denial of soul and functions of soul in animals; and second, empiricists blazed a new trail, partially indebted to Descartes, by shifting analysis from beast-machine to man-machine.

28. See Tom Regan, "The Moral Basis of Vegetarianism," *Canadian Journal of Philosophy* 5 (October 1975): 183–85.

29. Nov. 23, 1646, in *Descartes: Philosophical Letters*, trans. Anthony Kenny (Oxford: Oxford University Press, 1970).

30. Ibid., Feb. 5, 1649.

31. John Cottingham, "'A Brute to the Brutes?': Descartes' Treatment of Animals," *Philosophy* 53 (1978): 551–59.

32. Passmore, "Treatment of Animals," p. 205. Also see Singer, *Animal Liberation*, p. 219. Another theological problem that Descartes may be responding to is the question of whether animals, if they suffered, would have to

be assigned immortal souls. Although a surprising amount of human behavior was automatic as well for Descartes, this problem would not arise
with respect to human beings, in that it was clear to Descartes that human
beings had minds and immortal souls.

33. St. Augustine, The Free Choice of the Will, trans. F. P. Russell, in The Fa-
    thers of the Church series (Washington, D.C., 1968), vol. LIX, p. 227.

34. See, e.g., Immanuel Kant, "Duties to Animals and Spirits," in Lectures on
    Ethics, trans. Louis Infield (New York: Harper and Row, 1963), pp. 239–41.

35. Ibid.

36. Alexander Broadie and Elizabeth M. Pybus, "Kant's Treatment of Ani-
    mals," Philosophy 49 (October 1974): 375–83. Also see Christina Hoff,
    "Kant's Invidious Humanism," Environmental Ethics 5 (1983): 63–70; my
    review of this article will appear in Ethics & Animals.

37. Again, see Lectures on Ethics. Also see Devine, "Moral Basis of Vegetari-
    anism," pp. 502–3; and Passmore, "Treatment of Animals," p. 196.

38. Broadie and Pybus, "Kant's Treatment of Animals," p. 375. Also see an ar-
    ticle by the same authors, "Kant and the Maltreatment of Animals," Phi-
    losophy 53 (1978): 560–61.

39. Robert Nozick asks precisely this question. See Anarchy, State, and Uto-
    pia (New York: Basic Books, 1974), p. 39.

40. Singer, Animal Liberation, p. 227.

41. Again, see Montaigne, "Apology for Raimond de Sebonde"; Voltaire, "Ani-
    mals," in Philosophical Dictionary; Peter Singer's discussion of Emile in
    Animal Liberation, pp. 221–22; Michael J. Seidler, "Hume and the Ani-
    mals," Southern Journal of Philosophy 15 (Fall 1977): 361–72; Arthur
    Schopenhauer, On the Basis of Morality, trans. E. F. J. Payne (Indianapo-
    lis: Bobbs-Merrill, 1965), chap. 8, 19. Also see Singer, Animal Liberation,
    p. 229.

42. See Jeremy Bentham, The Principles of Morals and Legislation (1789),
    chap. XVII, sec. 1. Also see a defense of Bentham by John Stuart Mill in an
    essay titled "Whewell on Moral Philosophy," in Mill's Collected Works,
    vol. X, pp. 185–87.

43. Robert Nozick, Anarchy, State, and Utopia, p. 40. Also see Tom Regan,
    "Animal Rights, Human Wrongs," Environmental Ethics 2 (1980): 104–5,
    for a treatment of Kant; pp. 108–12 on utilitarianism.

44. Charles Darwin, The Descent of Man, chap. III, IV. Darwin's comparison of
    men with "higher" mammals would seem to warrant differential treat-
    ment among the various animal species, as we shall see.

45. Singer, Animal Liberation, pp. 224–26, 231.

46. See Robert S. Brumbaugh, "Man, Animals, and Morals: A Brief History,"
    in Richard Knowles Morris, ed., On the Fifth Day: Animal Rights and Hu-
    man Ethics (Washington, D.C.: Acropolis Press, 1978), for a thoughtful
    treatment of Descartes, Boyle, Leibniz, Locke, Kant, utilitarianism, and

the theory of evolution. Also see Ambrose Aquis, *God's Animals* (London: Catholic Study for Animal Welfare, 1970); George Boas, *The Happy Beast in French Thought of the Seventeenth Century* (New York: Octagon Books, 1966); Gerald Carson, *Men, Beasts, and Gods: A History of Cruelty and Kindness to Animals* (New York: Scribner's, 1972); and Jon Lowry, "Natural Rights: Men and Animals," *Southwestern Journal of Philosophy* 6 (Summer 1975).

2 The Golden Age

1. Stephen R. L. Clark, *The Moral Status of Animals*, p. 34.
2. Very helpful in the development of this chapter has been Arthur O. Lovejoy and George Boas, *Primitivism and Related Ideas in Antiquity* (New York: Octagon Books, 1965), pp. 24–31.
3. Hesiod, fragment 82 (216), Rzach, Leipzig, 1902. See also, e.g., many passages in the *Republic* (416E) and *Laws* (625C).
4. Johannes Haussleiter, *Der Vegetarismus in der antike*, I, 3, 4.
5. Ibid., I, 6. W. H. D. Rouse, *Gods, Heroes and Men of Ancient Greece* (New York: Mentor Books, 1957) relates other stories from Greek mythology which indicate the prevalence of anthropophagy: Lycaon fed human flesh to Zeus, who struck him with a thunderbolt out of anger (p. 51); and Tantalos fed his own son Pelops to the gods, who punished Tantalos, as is well known, in Hades (p. 143). Further, the Stymphalian birds ate human flesh, as did the horses of Diomedes (pp. 62–63). And the centaur Pholos ate his meat raw, even if it was not human flesh (p. 61). One can see why Rouse claims that Orpheus learned the wisdom of the gods by his journey to Hades when he became a vegetarian, at least when this anthropophagous background is considered (p. 145). Also, on the Orphics and Homer, see Evelyn Martinengo Cesaresco, "The Greek Conception of Animals," *Contemporary Review* 85 (1904): 430–39. Meat was not the constant diet of the Homeric Greeks because the idea of killing animals was still closely tied to religious sacrifice. This author also treats Aesop's tale of the "Lion's Kingdom," which alludes to the golden age. Finally, see Marcel Detienne, *Dionysus Slain*, trans. M. Muellner and L. Muellner (Baltimore: Johns Hopkins Press, 1979), where the author examines the Dionysus myth where the child god is slain, boiled and roasted, and consumed by the Titans, only to be reborn. The Orphic and Pythagorean devotees abstained from meat because, among other reasons, it reproduced the Titan's crime. On the other hand, the Dionysian and Cynic proponents of the myth saw it as a commendable rejection of civilization. Detienne also deals at length with the difference between eating meat raw or roasted, on the one hand, and boiled, on the other; the latter represented a higher gastronomic dimension.

6. Hermann Diels, *Fragmente der Vorsokratiker*, 4th ed. (Berlin, 1922), I, 271–72, fragment 128.

7. Ibid., I, 273, fragment 130.

8. Once again, Lovejoy and Boas are instructive, pp. 32–34.

9. Alexander Pope, *Essay on Man*, III, 147–60.

10. *Cratylus* 397, *Republic* 369, Book Three of the *Laws*, et al. For a full treatment of Plato's thought on history, see my *Plato's Philosophy of History* (Washington, D.C.: University Press of America, 1981). A review of the book by Charles Hartshorne can be found in *Process Studies* 12 (1982): 201–2.

11. *Plato's Philosophy of History*, chapter 7.

12. Pierre Vidal-Naquet, "Plato's Myth of the Statesman, the Ambiguities of the Golden Age and of History," *Journal of Hellenic Studies* XCVIII (1978): 132–41.

13. Again, I can only direct the reader to my *Plato's Philosophy of History* if this contention seems unsupported.

14. Ibid., pp. 48, 121, 134, especially regarding the treatment of Prometheus in the *Protagoras*.

15. Vidal-Naquet, "Plato's Myth," pp. 133–34.

16. Marcel Detienne, "Entre bêtes et Dieux," *Nouvelle Revue de Psychanalyse* VI (Autumn 1972): 230–46.

17. For example, read about the "MOVE Controversy" in Philadelphia in 1978.

18. See Vidal-Naquet, "Plato's Myth," p. 135. Also, for Antisthenes, see Diogenes Laertius, *Lives of Eminent Philosophers*, Greek with English trans. by R. D. Hicks (New York: Putnam, 1925), VI, 16–17; for Diogenes, see Diogenes Laertius, VI, 80.

19. See Diogenes Laertius, VI, 104.

20. See Porphyry's *De abstinentia*, II, 5–7, for a description of Theophrastus's thoughts in his *On Piety* (*Peri Eusebeias*). Also see Vidal-Naquet, "Plato's Myth," pp. 132–33; and Haussleiter, *Der Vegetarismus*, I, 8. Some comment is in order regarding my use of late classical sources in chapters 2 and 3. My treatment of the Cynics, Theophrastus, Dicaerchus, and the Pythagoreans relies heavily on such sources. Because Pythagoras left us nothing in writing, some sort of indirect approach is needed when he is considered; it will be seen in the next chapter that I use standard sources to decipher what his vegetarianism consisted in. And no harm is done, but much is accomplished, by using late classical sources in this chapter, because little in these sources conflicts with the more numerous sources I have used, which are *not* from the late classical period, yet which attest to the ancient belief in a vegetarian golden age: Homer, Hesiod, Empedocles, Plato, Strabo, Aratus, Diodorus Siculus, and Ovid. I also allow Plotinus to speak for himself. Finally, the later classical source I rely on most, Porphyry, happens to be far more reliable than the chatty Diogenes Laertius.

21. Porphyry, *De abstinentia*, IV, 2. Also see Vidal-Naquet, "Plato's Myth," p. 132; and Haussleiter, *Der Vegetarismus*, I, 8.

22. See Aristotle's *Rhetoric* 1364A.

23. Some in the modern debate do not shy away from calling man's current attack on animals a war. See, e.g., Clark, *Moral Status of Animals*, "war" in index.

24. Lovejoy and Boas, *Primitivism*, pp. 93–96.

25. See Cicero, *Tusculanae disputationes*, I, 10, 21. Also see *De officiis*, II, 5, fragment 67.

26. I am using the word "psychology" loosely so as to include those, like Dicaerchus, who deny the existence of souls.

27. Lovejoy and Boas, *Primitivism*, p. 93.

28. Ibid., pp. 287–90.

29. Vidal-Naquet, "Plato's Myth," p. 133. We know about Ephorus's treatment of the Scythians through Strabo, *Geography*, VII, 3, 9.

30. Lovejoy and Boas, *Primitivism*, pp. 287–88. See *Iliad* XIII, 3 ff., where Zeus views the noble mare-milkers and milk-drinking Abioi as the most righteous of men. Also Haussleiter, *Der Vegetarismus*, I, 6.

31. Aratus, *Phaenomena*, 96–136. See Lovejoy and Boas, *Primitivism*, pp. 34–36.

32. The following poem by Jane Legge is more a commentary on education than vegetarian propaganda. The poem is found in Cora Diamond, "Eating Meat and Eating People," *Philosophy* 53 (1978): 472–73:

> *Learning to be a Dutiful Carnivore*
> Dogs and cats and goats and cows,
> Ducks and chickens, sheep and sows
> Woven into tales for tots,
> Pictured on their walls and pots.
> Time for dinner! Come and eat
> All your lovely juicy meat.
> One day ham from Percy Porker
> (In the comics he's a corker),
> Then the breast from Mrs. Cluck
> Or the wing from Donald Duck.
> Liver next from Clara Cow
> (No, it doesn't hurt her now).
> Yes, that leg's from Peter Rabbit
> Chew it well; make that a habit.
> Eat the creatures killed for sale,
> But never pull the pussy's tail.
> Eat the flesh from "filthy hogs"
> But never be unkind to dogs.

> Grow up into double-think—
> Kiss the hamster; skin the mink.
> Never think of slaughter, dear,
> That's why animals are here.
> They only come on earth to die,
> So eat your meat, and don't ask why.

33. Diodorus Siculus, *Bibliotheca historica*, I, 8. See Lovejoy and Boas, *Primitivism*, pp. 220–21.

34. This sort of social contract, established out of self-interest or fear, has a long history from Book Two of the *Republic* to Rawls.

35. As has been noted, some Cynics also viewed primitive man negatively, but they did not see him as a vegetarian. Homer's view of Polyphemus might be another exception, to the extent that the land of the Cyclops was in a golden age.

36. See *Metamorphoses*, I, 76–215, and II, 17. Also see Lovejoy and Boas, *Primitivism*, pp. 43–50; and Haussleiter, *Der Vegetarismus*, I, 8, who reminds us that Ovid was a neo-Pythagorean.

37. J. Baird Callicott, "Animal Liberation: A Triangular Affair," *Environmental Ethics* 2 (1980): 311–38. Callicott relies on Aldo Leopold's notion of a "land ethic." It should be noted that although the word "ecology" has Greek roots (*oikos*=habitat; *logos*=rational inquiry), the Greeks never coined the word *oikologia*. Natural historians in the nineteenth century did this. See J. Donald Hughes, "Ecology in Ancient Greece," *Inquiry* 18 (1975): 115–25.

38. John Passmore, "The Treatment of Animals," p. 197.

39. See Lovejoy and Boas, *Primitivism*, p. 43.

40. I have borrowed this phrase from A. H. Armstrong. See *Enneads* V.1.4; V.1.7; V.5.3; and V.8.13.

41. See Stanley Godlovitch's article in *Animals, Men, and Morals*, ed. Stanley Godlovitch, Roslind Godlovitch, and John Harris, pp. 180–90.

42. See Singer, *Animal Liberation*, pp. 96–170.

3 The Pythagoreans

1. Tom Regan, "McCloskey on Why Animals Cannot Have Rights," *Philosophical Quarterly* 26 (July 1976): 251.

2. See Peter Gorman, *Pythagoras: A Life* (London: Routledge and Kegan Paul, 1979), pp. 36, 60, 113. The similarity between Orpheus and Pythagoras can be seen when one considers II, 36 of Porphyry's *De abstinentia*. E. Wynne-Tyson, editor of Porphyry, *On Abstinence from Animal Food*, trans. Thomas Taylor (London: Centaur Press, 1965), thinks that in this text Porphyry is referring to Orpheus. Yet J. Bouffartigue and M. Patillon, eds.,

Porphyre de l'abstinence (Paris, 1977), vol. 2, p. 11, think that Pythagoras is meant as the one prohibiting animal sacrifice in this text.

3. Herodotus, II, 123. Also see Wynne-Tyson, *On Abstinence*, p. 15, who holds that the priests of Isis taught Pythagoras about purification of soul.

4. Herodotus, II, 37.

5. Tom Regan, "The Moral Basis of Vegetarianism," *Canadian Journal of Philosophy* 5 (October 1975): 183.

6. Gorman, *Pythagoras*, pp. 60–61. Also see Johannes Haussleiter, *Der Vegetarismus in der antike*, II, 10.

7. Gorman, *Pythagoras*, pp. 32–36.

8. Ibid., pp. 8, 66–68. Also see Diogenes Laertius, I, 6–8.

9. See Haussleiter, *Der Vegetarismus*, II, 10; Diogenes Laertius, VIII, 33; and Wynne-Tyson, *On Abstinence*, p. 7.

10. Diogenes Laertius, VIII, 4, 5; Porphyry, *Life of Pythagoras*, 19, found in Moses Hadas and Morton Smith, eds., *Heroes and Gods* (New York: Harper and Row); Iamblichus, *Life of Pythagoras*, 14, trans. Thomas Taylor (London: Valpy, 1818).

11. Porphyry, *Life of Pythagoras*, 45, 22.

12. Ibid., 34–36. Parentheses 1, 2, and 4 are mine: parentheses 3 and 5 are in the text.

13. Iamblichus, *Life of Pythagoras*, 11.

14. Gorman, *Pythagoras*, p. 84.

15. Porphyry, *Life of Pythagoras*, 42–43.

16. Diogenes Laertius, VIII, 19–44; also see Porphyry, *Life of Pythagoras*, 45, about sea-wombs and anemones.

17. Although these abstinences were prescribed by those who performed the mystic rites in the temples, one should notice that some contemporary vegetarians also avoid eggs, but for a different reason, i.e., because of the brutality of contemporary farming in the poultry industry. See Peter Singer, *Animal Liberation: A New Ethics for Our Treatment of Animals* (New York: New York Review, 1975), pp. 100–118.

18. Ibid., p. 205.

19. Diogenes Laertius, VIII, 36.

20. Iamblichus, *Life of Pythagoras*, 26.

21. Act IV, Scene 2. This incident is reported in John Passmore, "The Treatment of Animals," *Journal of the History of Ideas* 36 (1975): 216.

22. See Porphyry, *De abstinentia*, I, 15.

23. Porphyry, *Life of Pythagoras*, 7.

24. See Gorman, *Pythagoras*, pp. 109–10, 206; Iamblichus, *Life of Pythagoras*, 8; Porphyry, *Life of Pythagoras*, 25.

25. Diogenes Laertius, VIII, 5; Porphyry, *Life of Pythagoras*, 45.

26. Iamblichus, *Life of Pythagoras*, 13; Porphyry, *Life of Pythagoras*, 23–25; also see Gorman, *Pythagoras*, pp. 110–11.

27. Haussleiter, *Der Vegetarismus*, II, 10.

28. See Iamblichus, *Life of Pythagoras*, 18, 28; also Diogenes Laertius, VIII, 34.

29. Iamblichus, *Life of Pythagoras*, 5, 7.

30. Diogenes Laertius, VIII, 13.

31. Iamblichus, *Life of Pythagoras*, 19, 28; Porphyry, *Life of Pythagoras*, 25.

32. See James Rachels, "Vegetarianism and 'The Other Weight Problem'," in *World Hunger and Moral Obligation*, ed. W. Aiken and H. LaFollette (Englewood Cliffs, N.J.: Prentice-Hall, 1977).

33. See Gorman, *Pythagoras*, p. 182.

34. Porphyry, *Life of Pythagoras*, 35.

35. Richard Rorty, *Philosophy and the Mirror of Nature* (Princeton: Princeton University Press, 1979), especially chap. 1.

36. Iamblichus, *Life of Pythagoras*, 31.

37. Diogenes Laertius, VIII, 13.

38. Iamblichus, *Life of Pythagoras*, 3.

39. Porphyry, *Life of Pythagoras*, 15. Also see Porphyry, *De abstinentia*, I, 26.

40. Diogenes Laertius, VIII, 12–13; Iamblichus, *Life of Pythagoras*, 5.

41. See Gorman, *Pythagoras*, pp. 106–7.

42. Diogenes Laertius, VIII, 34. Also see Thomas Taylor, trans., Iamblichus, *Life of Pythagoras*, op. cit., where Taylor suggests, citing Aristotle, that the bean, of all spermatic plants, is not obstructed by any intervening joints; this is why it resembles the gates of Hades (p. 295).

43. Porphyry, *Life of Pythagoras*, 44. Also see Gorman, *Pythagoras*, p. 37.

44. For example, Iamblichus, *Life of Pythagoras*, 31. Also see John Scarborough, "Beans, Pythagoras, Taboos, and Ancient Dietetics," *Classical World* 75 (1982): 355–58. This author reviews the studies of favism, many of which suggest that the Pythagorean prohibition of beans was due to medical reasons (e.g., Brumbaugh and Schwartz).

45. Diogenes, Laertius, VIII, 19, 34; Iamblichus, *Life of Pythagoras*, 33, 34.

46. Porphyry, *Life of Pythagoras*, 39.

47. Iamblichus, *Life of Pythagoras*, 30, 32; also see Taylor, in Iamblichus, *Life of Pythagoras*, where Taylor states that Pythagoras believed that some animals even possessed ethical virtues (p. 340).

48. Peter Gorman, *Pythagoras*, pp. 185, 202. Also see a popular article, "Pythagorean Objections against Animal Food," *London Magazine* (November 1825): 380–83.

49. Iamblichus, *Life of Pythagoras*, 28.

50. Ibid., 18, 20–22, 24. Also see Gorman, *Pythagoras*, pp. 125–30. Gorman believes that Iamblichus's account is taken from Aristotle and Timaeus, not Aristoxenus, who will be treated later. On the discussion of eating and spirituality that follows, see my "Eating and Spiritual Exercises: Food for Thought from Saint Ignatius and Nikos Kazantzakis," to appear in *Christianity and Literature* in 1983.

51. Gorman, *Pythagoras*, pp. 79, 108.

52. Marcel Detienne, "La Cuisine de Pythagore," *Archives de Sociologie des Religions* 29 (1970): 141–62.

53. Also in agreement with my sources is Apollonius of Tyana. See Gorman, *Pythagoras*, pp. 60, 75.

54. See, e.g., Diogenes Laertius, VIII, 20, for a treatment of Aristoxenus.

55. See Gorman, *Pythagoras*, pp. 6, 75, 190, 191. Aristoxenus's materialism would necessarily give him a different perspective from Timaeus.

56. Ibid., p. 102.

57. Iamblichus, *Life of Pythagoras*, 24.

58. Detienne, "La Cuisine de Pythagore," pp. 145, 147.

59. Ibid., pp. 148, 151; Detienne relies on D. Sabattucci here. See *Saggio sul misticismo greco* (Rome, 1965), pp. 69–83.

60. Detienne, "La Cuisine de Pythagore," pp. 152–55.

61. See Porphyry, *De abstinentia*, I, 36. My conclusion is not at all opposed to the positions of Gorman or Detienne.

62. Haussleiter, *Der Vegetarismus*, II, 10.

63. Diogenes Laertius, VIII, 23.

64. Ibid., 28, 30. Diogenes Laertius offers no criteria for distinguishing in this instance between *nous* and *phren*; perhaps he means by *nous* consciousness and by *phren* reflective consciousness that is capable of striving for *sophia*. But this is merely a guess. It is interesting to contrast Plato, who puts *nous* above all other capacities.

65. Porphyry, *Life of Pythagoras*, 39.

66. J. Donald Hughes, "The Environmental Ethics of the Pythagoreans," *Environmental Ethics* 3 (1980): 195–213; also see Strabo, *Geography*, trans. H. L. Jones, VII, 3, 5.

67. Ibid., p. 196.

68. See, e.g., the Pythagorean Philolaus, fragment 14 in Diels. Also see pp. 204–10 of Hughes's article, which deals with the similarities between Pythagorean attitudes (including vegetarianism) and primitive hunting culture, however strange these two may seem at first. Both see the natural world alive with spiritual forces, etc. Hughes, "Environmental Ethics."

69. Porphyry, *De abstinentia*, II, 36. For the most part, at least, the Pythagoreans avoided animal sacrifice.

70. Porphyry, *Life of Pythagoras*, 35.

71. Ibid., 49–50.

72. Diels, fragments 8–9.

73. Ibid., fragments 130, 77–78. Also see Detienne, "La Cuisine de Pythagore," p. 162.

74. Hughes, "Environmental Ethics," p. 201, cites Aristotle, *De plantis* 815A15, B17.

75. Diogenes Laertius, VIII, 77.

76. See Gorman, *Pythagoras*, p. 58. Also Diels, fragment 117.
77. Porphyry, *De abstinentia*, I, 3, and II, 21. Porphyry notices the strangeness of Empedocles' position, but does not state reasons why he thinks it strange. We will see in chapter 7 that there may still be another reason to be a vegetarian even if plants are sentient due to the degree and intensity of sentience in animals with central nervous systems.
78. Ibid., III, 6; J. Baird Callicott, "Animal Liberation: A Triangular Affair," p. 312.
79. John Rodman, "The Other Side of Ecology in Ancient Greece: Comments on Hughes," *Inquiry* 19 (1976): 108–12. Ovid's vegetarian thought also seems to have been inspired by Pythagoras; see *Metamorphoses*, XV, 60–480. He identifies Pythagoras as the first opponent to meat-eating; the criminality (*scelus*) of meat-eating is even compared to the savagery of the Cyclops or of a Thyestean banquet. Although Ovid is not opposed to killing animals that are dangerous, sheep and other harmless animals do not merit death, nor do they deserve to be eaten by savage teeth (*vulnera dente*), or caught in treacherous (*timentia*) snares. In the golden age the infamy (*nefas*) of meat-eating was avoided, so there was no need to make the gods partners in human lust (*fames*) for forbidden food. Also, Ovid's comparison of the slaying of a kid with the cry of a child anticipates the argument from marginal cases, which can be seen explicitly in Porphyry. Finally, see Antonio Cocci, *The Pythagorean Diet of Vegetables Only* (London, 1745).

4 Socrates through Theophrastus

1. Diogenes Laertius, IX, 3.
2. Porphyry, *De abstinentia*, I, 15; Johannes Haussleiter, *Der Vegetarismus in der antike* (Berlin: Topelmann, 1935), III, 12. The chronology of Plato's dialogues that I am using follows those of Taylor and Ross. Only Plato's early dialogues are meant to depict the thought of Socrates, dialogues which include the *Laches* and *Lesser Hippias*, which I have used on Socrates. Although the *Symposium* is a middle dialogue, it contains biographical items on Socrates which are generally used to describe him; the same is true of the *Phaedo*. I have supplemented information in Plato on Socrates with other sources, including Xenophon's account, which is especially informative on Socrates and animals. Using the evidence from the middle and late dialogues, I will develop a somewhat different picture of Plato. Although the authenticity of the *Epinomis* has been questioned, see a strong argument for its authenticity in A. E. Taylor, "Plato and the Authorship of the *Epinomis*," *Proceedings of the British Academy* XV (1929): 235–318.

3. Diogenes Laertius, II, 34.

4. See Xenophon, *Recollections of Socrates*, trans. Anna S. Benjamin (Indianapolis: Bobbs-Merrill, 1965), I, 2; II, 1.

5. Ibid., I, 3.

6. Ibid., I, 6; II, 1.

7. Some contemporary philosophers have argued that one important way to ameliorate the plight of the hungry man is through a vegetarian diet in wealthy nations, which would save an incredible amount of grain for others. See, e.g., James Rachels, "Vegetarianism and 'The Other Weight Problem'," in *World Hunger and Moral Obligation*, ed. W. Aiken and H. LaFollette (Englewood Cliffs, N.J.: Prentice-Hall, 1977). This argument from protein efficiency was obviously beyond the bounds of anything Socrates could have thought of.

8. Xenophon, III, 14.

9. Ibid., II, 1.

10. Ibid., I, 4.

11. Ibid., IV, 3. Also see Xenophon's "On the Art of Horsemanship" and "On Hunting."

12. Diogenes Laertius, II, 122, 71.

13. Haussleiter, *Der Vegetarismus*, III, 13.

14. Diogenes Laertius, II, 68; VI, 29; VI, 37, 61. The figs were eaten off a tree that a man hung himself on. This did not bother Diogenes. It should be remembered, however, that some of the Cynics desired to eat every kind of food, see Porphyry, *De abstinentia*, I, 42.

15. Diogenes Laertius, VI, 57. Diogenes supposedly chided Plato as well; see VI, 25. Curiously enough, because Plato's position on the eating of animals is unclear at this point, he was eating olives and figs when chided.

16. Ibid., VI, 69. Diogenes viewed his stomach as a monstrous Charybdis; see VI, 51.

17. Ibid., VI, 85.

18. Ibid., VI, 94.

19. In addition to these passages from the *Gorgias*, see Diogenes Laertius, III, 85.

20. Ibid., III, 90.

21. John Rodman, "The Other Side of Ecology in Ancient Greece: Comments on Hughes," *Inquiry* 19 (1976): 110.

22. Peter Singer, *Animal Liberation: A New Ethics for Our Treatment of Animals* (New York: New York Review, 1975), p. 216.

23. Haussleiter, *Der Vegetarismus*, III, 14. Also see F. M. Cornford, "Plato and Orpheus," *The Classical Review* XVII (1903): 433–45; and *Republic* 620A.

24. Peter Gorman, *Pythagoras: A Life* (London: Routledge and Kegan Paul, 1978), p. 76.

25. See J. Baird Callicott, "Animal Liberation: A Triangular Affair," *Environmental Ethics* 2 (1980): 327–28.
26. Diogenes Laertius, II, 129, 132, 139, 143.
27. Ibid., IV, 1, 10, 17; IX, 66–68.
28. Singer, *Animal Liberation*, p. 207.
29. A brief consideration of three authors will indicate what some of these problems are. G. E. R. Lloyd, "The Development of Aristotle's Theory of the Classification of Animals," *Phronesis* 6 (1961): 59–81, argues that Aristotle started out using the Platonic method of division, then criticized this method in favor of a more empirical one. D. M. Balme, "Aristotle's Use of Differentiae in Zoology," in *Articles on Aristotle*, vol. 1, ed. J. Barnes, M. Schofield, and R. Sorabji (London: Duckworth, 1975), pp. 183–93, sees Aristotle's procedure in animal classification as a reformed Academic one which could not be other than inductive. But Aristotle's intent in the *History of Animals* is not to use differentiae to classify animals at all; rather it is to study the differences themselves among animals. Balme shows great optimism in the preface to his translations of *On the Parts of Animals* and *On the Generation of Animals* (Oxford: Clarendon Press, 1972), when he says there is disagreement among scholars only over details in these works and not over "major issues." Not only is there (major?) disagreement between Balme and Lloyd, but also between both and Johannes Morsink, *Aristotle on the Generation of Animals* (Washington, D.C.: University Press of America, 1982), who argues that Aristotle is much less a Baconian than we have taken him to be; in fact, Morsink sees Aristotle making Popperian conjectures and refutations. I am glad I do not have to decide among these interpretations.
30. Book II, chap. 3: 414A28–415A10.
31. Also see *On the Parts of Animals*, Book I, chap. 1: 641A35–641B10.
32. Joseph Margolis, "Animals Have No Rights and Are Not the Equal of Humans," *Philosophic Exchange* 1 (1974): 119–23.
33. See Pamela M. Huby, "The Epicureans, Animals, and Free-will," *Apeiron* 3 (January 1969): 19; and David J. Furley, "Self-Movers," in *Essays on Aristotle's Ethics*, ed. Amélie Oksenberg Rorty (Berkeley: University of California Press, 1980), pp. 55–67.
34. Porphyry, *De abstinentia*, III, 6, 8, 9, and 12.
35. See, e.g., Peter Jenkins, "Teaching Chimpanzees to Communicate." On instinct see Mary Midgley, "The Concept Of Beastliness." Both articles are in Tom Regan and Peter Singer, eds., *Animal Rights and Human Obligations* (Englewood Cliffs, N.J.: Prentice-Hall, 1976).
36. See Singer, *Animal Liberation*, p. 206.
37. Henry S. Salt, "Animal Rights," in Tom Regan and Peter Singer, *Animal Rights and Human Obligations*, p. 174.
38. See W. Wieland, "The Problem of Teleology," in *Articles on Aristotle*, vol.

1, ed. J. Barnes, M. Schofield, and R. Sorabji, p. 158. Also see Martha Craven Nussbaum, *Aristotle's De Motu Animalium* (Princeton: Princeton University Press, 1978), pp. 59–60.

39. Regan and Singer, *Animal Rights and Human Obligations*, pp. 3–4. Also see Stewart Richards, "Forethoughts for Carnivores," *Philosophy* 56 (1981): 75, 78–79. The author notices that although few, if any, of the characteristics listed by Aristotle as indicators of the uniqueness of man now stand, Aristotle did correctly attribute pain to animals in two senses: (1) a direct consequence of some physical insult; and (2) an indirect consequence of psychological suffering as the form of sensations deprived of matter. Finally, see George Boas, "Theriophily," *Dictionary of the History of Ideas* (1973), IV, p. 384.

40. Rodman, "The Other Side of Ecology," p. 111.

41. Gareth B. Matthews, "Animals and the Unity of Psychology," *Philosophy* 53 (October 1978): 439.

42. 588A18–B3.

43. See Nussbaum, *Aristotle's De Motu*, p. 347.

44. See T. H. Irwin, "The Metaphysical and Psychological Basis of Aristotle's Ethics," in Amélie Oksenberg Rorty, ed., *Essays on Aristotle's Ethics*.

45. Hughes, "Ecology in Ancient Greece," pp. 122–24.

46. Diogenes Laertius, V, 43–44, 49.

47. Hughes's designation.

48. See, e.g., *Enquiry into Plants* and *Causes of Plants*, Loeb edition.

49. See George Malcolm Stratton for a treatment of the issue of pleasure and pain in *De Sensibus*; see his *Theophrastus and the Greek Physiological Psychology Before Aristotle* (New York: Macmillan, 1917), pp. 48–50.

50. Haussleiter, *Der Vegetarismus*, IV, 19.

51. Ibid.

5   The Hellenistic Era

1. John Passmore, "The Treatment of Animals," *Journal of the History of Ideas* 36 (1975): 198, 208. My order of treatment in this chapter is, in a peculiar way, chronological. I start with the Stoics, who were originally Greek, but who had many Roman adherents, like Cicero. I also treat here some criticisms of Stoicism from later figures like Porphyry. Second, I treat Epicurus and his followers; third, the Romans who were not Stoics; and finally, Plutarch. And Max Pohlenz, *Die Stoa* (Göttingen, 1948), p. 137, 147; quoted in Passmore, "Treatment of Animals," p. 198; and pp. 204, 208.

2. For example, Cicero, *De natura deorum* II, 14, 37. Also see Stephen R. L. Clark, *The Moral Status of Animals* (Oxford: Clarendon Press, 1977), p. 15.

3. For example, Cicero, *De officiis* I, 50–51. And Clark, *Moral Status of Animals*, p. 25. This Stoic conception of justice obviously relies heavily

on Aristotle's treatments in the *Nichomachean Ethics* of justice and friendship.

4. See J. W. Jones, *Law and Legal Theory of the Greeks* (Oxford, 1956), pp. 61–62. Also see S. L. Pembroke, "*Oikeiosis*," in *Problems in Stoicism*, ed. A. A. Long (London, 1971), pp. 114 ff.

5. See Clark, *Moral Status of Animals*, pp. 34, 110, 197, 59.

6. Porphyry, *De abstinentia*, I, 4–6.

7. *Works and Days*, I, 5, 275; quoted in Porphyry, *De abstinentia*, I, 4–6.

8. Clark, *Moral Status of Animals*, pp. 17, 164, 169.

9. Porphyry, *De abstinentia*, III, 19–20.

10. The argument from sentiency, simply stated, goes something like this:

    A. Any being that can suffer at the very least has a right not to be forced to suffer unnecessarily.
    B. It is not necessary that we inflict suffering on animals so that we can eat, especially because eating vegetables can be very healthy.
    C. Therefore, to inflict unnecessary suffering on animals so as to eat them is morally reprehensible or cruel.

    Many of the ancient vegetarians argue in this fashion. The argument from marginal cases is a bit more complicated, and can be used effectively when the meat eater proposes to kill animals "painlessly." See Peter Singer, *Animal Liberation: A New Ethics for Our Treatment of Animals* (New York: New York Review, 1975), p. 265; and Tom Regan, "Fox's Critique of Animal Liberation," *Ethics* 88 (January 1978): 126–33. Singer's version goes as follows:

    The catch is that any such characteristic that is possessed by *all* human beings will not be possessed *only* by human beings. For example, all humans, but not only humans, are capable of feeling pain; and although only humans are capable of solving complex mathematical problems, not all humans can do this. So it turns out that in the only sense in which we can truly say, as an assertion of fact, that all humans are equal, at least some members of other species are also "equal"—equal, that is, to some humans.

    Or, as Regan puts it, if an animal has characteristics a, b, c . . . n but lacks autonomy (or reason or language) and a human being has characteristics a, b, c . . . n but lacks autonomy (or reason or language), then we have as much reason to believe that the animal has rights as the human.

11. Passmore, "Treatment of Animals," p. 204; Porphyry, *De abstinentia*, IV, 8.

12. Diogenes Laertius, VII, 13, 27. Diogenes Laertius makes it clear, however, at VII, 86 that Zeno's simple eating habits were more due to his anthropocentrism than opposed to it. This sort of eating will become more understandable when I treat Epicurus. Two other points should be added: (1) Di-

onysus of Heraclea, a student of Zeno's, committed suicide at age eighty by starving himself (VII, 167); and (2) there is some evidence that the Stoic Chrysippus was himself a fig-eater (VII, 185).

13. Haussleiter, *Der Vegetarismus*, V, 20–24.

14. See Epictetus, *Enchiridion*, XXIX, XXXIII. In this latter section Epictetus indicates that he does eat some meat.

15. Howard Williams, *The Ethics of Diet* (London: Richard James, 1907), pp. 40–43.

16. Epistle CXXI, Loeb edition.

17. Epistle CVIII, 27 ff. Also see Clark, *Moral Status of Animals*, p. 4.

18. Peter Gorman, *Pythagoras: A Life* (London: Routledge and Kegan Paul, 1978), p. 197.

19. Williams, *Ethics of Diet*, pp. 32–40.

20. Haussleiter, *Der Vegetarismus*, VI, 25.

21. Diogenes Laertius, X, 10–11.

22. Ibid., X, 150.

23. See Benjamin Farrington, *The Faith of Epicurus* (New York: Basic Books, 1967), pp. 12, 88, 127. There is little, if any, evidence that Epicurus advocated occasional "real" feasts. Also, Epicurus may have held to his vegetarian diet because of his bad stomach condition. Finally, it should be noted that a full treatment of Epicurus's views on animals would have to include his atomism and his view of the soul.

24. Porphyry, *De abstinentia*, I, 53.

25. On Lucretius see *De rerum natura*, Loeb ed., II, 991–99 and IV, 633–40. Also see S. F. Sapontzis, "Must We Value Life to Have a Right to It?" *Ethics & Animals* 3 (1982): 2–11. On Polystratus and Philodemus, see Johannes Haussleiter, VI, 26, and Diogenes Laertius, X, 25. On Hermarchus, see Porphyry, *De abstinentia*, I, 7–12.

26. Porphyry, *De abstinentia*, I, 48.

27. Robert S. Brumbaugh, "Man, Animals, and Morals: A Brief History," in *On the Fifth Day: Animal Rights and Human Ethics*, ed. Richard Knowles Morris, pp. 6–10.

28. See George Boas, "Theriophily," *Dictionary of the History of Ideas* (1973), p. 385 on Democritus.

29. Ibid., where Boas cites *Memorabilia*, I, iv, 2 and IV, iii, 9–12. Anaxagoras was also a believer in man's superiority, but not because of his intelligence: only man has laws, cities, etc.

30. Singer, *Animal Liberation*, p. 207.

31. W. E. H. Lecky, *History of European Morals from Augustus to Charlemagne* (London, 1869), I, 280–82. Also on the Romans see Evelyn Martinengo Cesaresco, who talks of the polar opposite to the golden age in "Animals at Rome," *Contemporary Review* 86 (1904): 225–34; H. H. Scullard, *The Elephant in the Greek and Roman World* (London: Thames and

Hudson, 1974); Jocelyn Toynbee, *Animals in Roman Life and Art* (Ithaca: Cornell University Press, 1973); R. E. Thomas, *The Sacred Meal in the Older Roman Religion* (University of Chicago Libraries, 1937); George Jennison, *Animals for Show and Pleasure in Ancient Rome* (Manchester: Manchester University Press, 1937); and H. Martin, "Plutarch's *De Sollertia Animalium*: The Discussion of the Encomium of Hunting," *American Journal of Philology* 100 (1979): 99–106.

32. Quoted in E. Wynne-Tyson, "Introduction," in Porphyry, *On Abstinence from Animal Food*, p. 10. Also see Singer, *Animal Liberation*, pp. 209–10. On Ovid, see my n. 79 in chapter 3.

33. See J. B. Moyle, trans., *Institutes of Justinian* (London, 1913), pp. 169–70. Also see Passmore, "Treatment of Animals," p. 206; See the long quote on p. 9 of Brumbaugh's article, "Man, Animals, and Morals: A Brief History," in *On the Fifth Day*.

34. Williams, *Ethics of Diet*, pp. 26–32; also pp. 1–10, 14–23.

35. Gorman, *Pythagoras*, p. 58.

36. R. H. Barrow, *Plutarch and His Times* (London: Chatto and Windus, 1967), p. 112. Also see Williams, *Ethics of Diet*, pp. 43–50; W. E. H. Lecky, *History of European Morals*, I, 244.

37. See Plutarch, "Consolation to His Wife"; also P. H. DeLacy, "Plutarch," *The Encyclopaedia of Philosophy*, ed. Paul Edwards (New York: Macmillan, 1967), VI, p. 360; and Singer, *Animal Liberation*, pp. 210–11.

38. Cf., John Benson, "Duty and the Beast," *Philosophy* 53 (1978): 529.

39. William H. Goodwin, ed., *Plutarch's Morals* (Boston: Little, Brown, and Co., 1870), 5 vols. This is the translation done by "several hands."

40. See Stewart Richards, "Forethoughts for Carnivores," *Philosophy* 56 (1981): 73–87.

41. Passmore, "Treatment of Animals," p. 207, notices that Plutarch always disapproves of meat-eating, even late in life, despite the fact that he makes some concessions to his custom-bound fellows.

42. Singer, *Animal Liberation*, p. 188. On the indifference of the utilitarian approach to the rationality of animals, see Passmore, "Treatment of Animals," p. 211.

43. The fact that Solon was an ancestor of Plato should not be forgotten.

44. Again, see Mary Midgley, "The Concept of Beastliness," in Tom Regan and Peter Singer, *Animal Rights and Human Obligations* (Englewood Cliffs, N.J.: Prentice-Hall, 1976).

45. See, e.g., "Down on the Factory Farm," in Singer, *Animal Liberation*; and Richard Ryder, "Experiments on Animals," in Tom Regan and Peter Singer, *Animal Rights and Human Obligations*. Unfortunately, some are still quite ignorant of the fact that on a modern farm chickens do not wander as they please, nor do cows chew happily until their death (much less *at* their death).

46. Singer, *Animal Liberation*.

47. See Clark, *Moral Status of Animals*, p. 189.

48. Boas, "Theriophily," pp. 384–85.

49. It is interesting how some anthropocentrists will go to all ends to obtain a fur coat, leather shoes or belt, etc., thereby going "in drag" as an animal.

50. This eating of raw meat, it should be noted, seems to be an exception to the rule for Diogenes, who is usually reported to have eaten simple, vegetal foods.

51. See Richard Ryder, "Experiments on Animals," in Tom Regan and Peter Singer, *Animal Rights and Human Obligations*. Also Singer, "Tools for Research," in *Animal Liberation*. These authors document how many, if not most, experiments that go on under the guise of "the benefit of humanity" are hardly contributions to that end.

52. Clark, *Moral Status of Animals*, p. 139.

53. *Odyssey*, X, 234.

54. Singer, *Animal Liberation*, pp. 127–35, 147–48; also pp. 49–55. Other documentation for these practices is easy to obtain.

55. Porphyry, *De abstinentia*, III, 18. Also see Passmore, "Treatment of Animals," p. 206, where the author notices that Plutarch grants to the Stoic that we can legitimately kill animals when necessary, but holds, against the Stoic, that this would force two conditions on us: (1) we would have to give up meat for the table; and (2) we would have to give up animal sports, e.g., hunting and animal fights.

56. See Plutarch's "Which Are the Most Crafty, Water or Land Animals?," 2.

57. See Euripides, *Cresphontes*, fragment 457.

58. With no explanation whatsoever, Harold Cherniss and William C. Helmbold contend that "these fragments probably depict faithfully a foible of Plutarch's early manhood." See *Plutarch's Moralia*, Loeb ed., vol. 12, p. 537. Because these writers dealt with this essay before the rebirth of the phoenix of philosophical vegetarianism their remarks can be excused; surely, they seem to be suggesting, Plutarch could never have been a vegetarian as a mature man. Realizing that vegetarianism can be a mature position is what these authors fail to see.

59. The two main characters, Autobulus and Soclarus, both seem to have Plutarch's support, as they are not so much opposed to each other as complementary to each other.

60. Also see Porphyry, *De abstinentia*, III, 24. Below, on the issue of infanticide, see George Willis Botsford, *Hellenic History* (New York: Macmillan, 1930), p. 409, for a description of how children exposed to the elements died, usually girls or deformed boys, in ancient Greece. While militating against human kindness, this practice contributed to the physical vitality of an athletic and military-oriented people. Even the Athenians sometimes engaged in the practice.

61. See Hughes, "Environmental Ethics," pp. 195–213; Clark, *Moral Status of Animals*, p. 124. Clark's many references to Plutarch can be found on pp. 17, 28, 73, 77, 82, 108, 118, 124, 128, 131, 138, 176, 189.

62. Barrow, *Plutarch*, p. 116.

63. Ibid., p. 117.

64. See Boas, "Theriophily," pp. 385–86, for the comic roots of Plutarch; and for Boas's reference to fragments of Philemon and Menander.

65. Ibid.; see Pliny, *Natural History*, VII, 1 of proemium.

66. G. B. Gelli's *Circe* (1549) picks up the theme of Plutarch's Gryllus dialogue. Also see Singer, *Animal Liberation*, pp. 221–22, where Rousseau is mentioned, whose *Émile* recognizes the strength of the vegetarian position, although Rousseau apparently did not adopt it. An extended treatment of the land-water animals dialogue and the piece on Gryllus can be found in James E. Gill, "Theriophily in Antiquity: A Supplementary Account," *Journal of the History of Ideas* 30 (1969): 401–12. Gill treats Lovejoy and Boas, whose notion of theriophily refers to the idea that animals are in some way superior to men. (Boas's article "Theriophily," in the *Dictionary of the History of Ideas*, treats the notion more broadly so as to include admiration for the ways of animals.) For Gill, the history of theriophily, in the sense of animal superiority, begins with Aristotle's *Historia animalium*, which gives animals greater intellectual powers in potentia than in *De anima*. Theophrastus learned this lesson well when he held that there are no qualitative distinctions with regard to either intellect or emotion between animals and men—see Theodor Gomperz, *Greek Thinkers: A History of Ancient Philosophy*, trans. Magnus and Berry (London, 1955), IV, p. 495. Menander was known to have been a student of Theophrastus. The Aristotelian origin of this type of theriophily is not odd when *Politics* 1253A is considered; for man, when perfected, is the best of animals, but when separated from law and justice he is the worst of all. The Stoics preserved the more dominant Aristotelian attitude toward animals through a distinction between *logos endiathetios* (the reason of the world) and *logos prophorikos* (the reason of human discourse). For Gill (also see Vernon Arnold, *Roman Stoicism* [Cambridge, 1911], p. 146), the loss of this distinction would enable, if not require, one to see animals as resembling human beings in important respects. In this regard, see Seneca, Epistle LXXIV. Skeptics like Sextus Empiricus rejected this distinction, not so much to give animals reason but to question the efficacy of human reason. Gill here gives us an important clue as to why the skeptical tradition up to Hume did not consistently hold to its position regarding animals by becoming vegetarians. See Sextus Empiricus, *Against the Logicians*, II, 287. Also notice the character of Cotta the Academic in Cicero's *De natura deorum*; Cotta anticipates Feuerbach's suggestion that if birds could theologize God would have feathers.

6 The Neoplatonists

1. Peter Singer, *Animal Liberation: A New Ethics for Our Treatment of Animals* (New York: New York Review, 1975), p. 173.

2. John Benson, "Duty and the Beast," *Philosophy* 53 (October 1978): 548.

3. See Peter Gorman, *Pythagoras: A Life* (London: Routledge and Kegan Paul, 1978) pp. 75, 189; also Johannes Haussleiter, *Der Vegetarismus in der antike* (Berlin: Topelmann, 1935), VII and VIII. Howard Williams, *The Ethics of Diet* (London: Richard James, 1907), pp. 68–70, adds to Haussleiter's treatment of Julian, the Christian emperor who was influenced by Neoplatonic vegetarianism. Julian writes about the difference between the vegetarian and flesh-eating diets:

    > Is not the former without life, the latter possessed of it? Is not the former pure, the latter full of blood and all that is unpleasing to the sight? The former, too, has the additional recommendation that no one is injured by the eating of it; whereas, in the other case, there is the slaughtering and throat-cutting of animals, who suffer pain thereby . . . and utter dreadful cries and moans.

    Unfortunately, this man eventually was corrupted by superstition and fanaticism, as Williams sees it, and offered sacrificial victims in the name of religion. For Apollonius of Tyana see, in addition to Haussleiter, Jean Bouffartigue and Michel Patillon, *Porphyre de l'abstinence* (Paris, 1977), vol. 2, p. 30; and Philostratus, *Life of Apollonius*, I, 8; VIII, 7.

4. See Émile Brehier, *The Philosophy of Plotinus*, trans. J. Thomas (Chicago: University of Chicago Press, 1958), pp. 106–31; and A. H. Armstrong, *The Architecture of the Intelligible Universe in the Philosophy of Plotinus* (Cambridge: Cambridge University Press, 1940).

5. I.1.11; IV.7.14; VI.4.16; VI.7.6.

6. I.4.1; III.3.3; III.4.1; IV.4.22; IV.4.27; IV.4.28; IV.9.1; V.2.2; VI.3.7.

7. I.4.1; III.4.2; IV.4.25; IV.4.26; IV.4.27; IV.9.1; V.2.2; VI.3.7.

8. III.2.9; III.3.3; III.8.1; IV.9.1; VI.7.5; VI.7.7; VI.7.8; VI.7.9.

9. For example, see III.2.9.

10. See E. Wynne-Tyson, "Introduction," Porphyry, *On Abstinence from Animal Food*, trans. T. Taylor (London: Centaur Press, 1965), p. 15.

11. IV.4.19; VI.8.2; IV.4.28; IV.9.3.

12. V.1.4; V.1.7; V.5.3; V.8.13.

13. Concerning Taylor, see John Passmore, "The Treatment of Animals," *Journal of the History of Ideas* 36 (1975): 207–8; and Singer, *Animal Liberation*, p. 1. My comment can go both ways. Singer's failure to note that Taylor translated *De abstinentia* indicates that modern vegetarians might profit from a reconsideration of Greek philosophy. See Porphyry, *On Abstinence from Animal Food*, trans. Thomas Taylor, edited with an introduc-

tion by E. Wynne-Tyson (London: Centaur Press, 1965). Even more recent than this new edition of Taylor's English translation is *Porphyre de l'abstinence*, trans. Jean Bouffartigue and Michel Patillon (Paris, 1977), 3 vols. Hereafter cited as BP. The introduction and notes of this edition, with Greek and French on facing pages, have been valuable in the development of this chapter.

14. Williams, *Ethics of Diet*, p. 64.
15. BP, vol. 1, p. xxii.
16. Williams, *Ethics of Diet*, p. 62.
17. Ibid., p. 64.
18. See M. J. Boyd, "*De abstinentia* I, 7–12," *Classical Quarterly* (1936): 188–91, on Porphyry's treatment of Epicureanism.
19. See Clark, *Moral Status of Animals*, p. 117.
20. Claudius is not the last person to use just war theory as a cover for other interests. Ibid., pp. 23, 28, in reference to III, 18, where God only forgives our necessities.
21. Ibid., p. 15. Also see Tom Regan and Peter Singer, *Animal Rights and Human Obligations* (Englewood Cliffs, N.J.: Prentice-Hall, 1976), p. 144, for Salt's treatment of swine and pearls.
22. Porphyry's vegetarianism is not an ivory tower affair, however. See BP, vol. 1, pp. liv, xxxv. True *theoria* consists in reasons (*logoi*) and action (*erga*). As in Book Six of the *Republic* the job of the philosopher is to both glance in the direction of the Good and to try to reform the city.
23. See Hermann Schöne, "*De abstinentia* I, 34," *Rheinisches Museum für Philologie* LXXIII: 443–48.
24. See Williams, *Ethics of Diet*, p. 66, where it is held that for Porphyry the one who extends his sympathies to all life is nearest the divine. The extent to which this works against divine simplicity and self-sufficiency, however, is not at all clear.
25. Clark, *Moral Status of Animals*, p. 177. Also see *De abstinentia*, IV, 21, where Porphyry suggests that Xenocrates was also opposed to animal sacrifices in favor of the fruits of the earth.
26. See Williams, *Ethics of Diet*, p. 67, for the relationship between Voltaire and Porphyry; According to BP, vol. 2, p. 4, Porphyry is heavily influenced by Theophrastus in Book Two. But BP do see some major differences between these two, pp. 19–20. For example, Porphyry's vegetarianism is oriented toward the individual in an atemporal way, whereas Theophrastus's analysis is social (like Singer's) and historical. Porphyry is interested in combating perversion of the soul, Theophrastus in combating perversion of custom. These contrasts, however, should not be overemphasized, especially when one sees the diversity of Porphyry's approaches. Also a bit too strongly put is the position of U. Dierauer, *Tier und Mensch im Denken der Antike* (Amsterdam, 1977), pp. 286–90. He distinguishes between two

types of vegetarianism: (1) that which wants to spare animals; and (2) that which is concerned with the soul of man. Porphyry is placed in the second category, with some justification, but Porphyry's belief in the rationality of animals and his sympathy for their suffering indicate that the first category is not outside his grasp.

27. Passmore, "Treatment of Animals," p. 211.

28. *History of Animals*, IV, 9; and *De anima*, II, 8.

29. BP, vol. 2, p. 135, deal with the "all or nothing" Aristotelian conception of reason; p. 139 deals with the influence of Philo on Porphyry's conception of animal rationality.

30. See Bernard E. Rollin, "Beasts and Men: The Scope of Moral Concern," *The Modern Schoolman* 55 (1978): 241–60, where the author treats a different conception of reason found in Kant. Although, for Kant (p. 248), there are different degrees of actualizing the rational faculty, there is only one (i.e., human) reason. Rollin notices (p. 253) that Kant's argument is circular; from the outset reason can only apply to beings that use language and make judgments like human beings.

31. See R. G. Collingwood, *The Idea of History* (New York: Galaxy Books, 1956), p. 227, for a discussion of how cats show the beginnings of historical understanding in the way they teach their young.

32. Konrad Lorenz, *On Aggression*, trans. M. Kerr (New York: Harcourt, Brace, and World, 1966). Also see Clark, *Moral Status of Animals*, p. 155, where the author holds that it is because we are animals that we display parental and familial care; and as Aristotle notices (*Nichomachean Ethics*, 8), it is out of family relationships that our sense of justice arises. Finally, see Clark's *The Nature of the Beast: Are Animals Moral?* (Oxford: Oxford University Press, 1982).

33. See BP, vol. 1, p. lviii, where the authors show that for Porphyry union with God is possible without death.

34. See E. Wynne-Tyson in Porphyry, *On Abstinence from Animal Food*, p. 163, for some notes on the Jews.

35. Also see Porphyry's treatment of the Syrians (15), Persians (16), and the Eleusinian mysteries (16).

7 *Arete*, Rorty and Hartshorne

1. I am relying to a large extent in the first part of this chapter on two articles by J. O. Urmson: "Saints and Heroes," in *Essays in Moral Philosophy*, ed. A. I. Melden (Seattle: University of Washington Press, 1958); and "Aristotle's Doctrine of the Mean," in *Essays on Aristotle's Ethics*, ed. Amélie Oksenberg Rorty. Obviously category (4) is the most controversial, but in that ultimately I do not place vegetarianism in this category, no harm will be done by examining it. Opponents to Urmson's treatment of super-

erogation include Elizabeth M. Pybus, "Saints and Heroes," *Philosophy* 57 (1982): 193–99; and Susan Wolf, "Moral Saints," *Journal of Philosophy* 79 (1982): 419–39. Pybus tries to collapse (4) into (3), and Wolf criticizes the very idea of moral excellence. Defenders of Urmson include Michael S. Pritchard, "Self-Regard and the Supererogatory," in *Respect for Persons*, ed. O. H. Green (New Orleans: Tulane University Press, 1982); Michael Clark, "The Meritorious and the Mandatory," *The Aristotelian Society* 79 (1978–79); and David Heyd, *Supererogation* (Cambridge: Cambridge University Press, 1982).

2. Henry David Thoreau, "Reform and the Reformers," in *Reform Papers*, ed. Wendell Glick (Princeton: Princeton University Press, 1973), p. 323.

3. Jan Narveson, "Animal Rights," *Canadian Journal of Philosophy* 7 (March 1977): 164.

4. Kai Nielsen, "Persons, Morals and the Animal Kingdom," *Man and World* 11 (1978): 233.

5. Stephen R. L. Clark, *The Moral Status of Animals*, (Oxford: Clarendon Press, 1977), p. 59.

6. This list is loosely based on Urmson, "Aristotle's Doctrine of the Mean," p. 158. The fact that we are using Aristotle for the purpose of defending vegetarianism should not bother us because, as Theophrastus shows, Aristotle may have been an inadequate interpreter of his own theories on animals. Also, Alastair MacIntyre has argued in *After Virtue* (South Bend, Ind.: University of Notre Dame Press, 1981) that an *arete*-based ethics includes duties as one component (p. 141). There is no reason in MacIntyre's book why refusal to eat animal flesh cannot be such a duty.

7. See Urmson, "Saints and Heroes," pp. 200–201. I am compressing Urmson's three types of heroism or sainthood into two types. It should also be noted that in "Aristotle's Doctrine of the Mean," p. 158, Urmson admits that we cannot distinguish (B) from (C) either by their actions or beliefs, but only by their desires.

8. Urmson, "Saints and Heroes," pp. 211, 213.

9. Tom Regan, "The Moral Basis of Vegetarianism," *Canadian Journal of Philosophy* 5 (1975): 182.

10. Ibid., p. 213, and Peter Singer, "The Fable of the Fox and the Unliberated Animals," *Ethics* 88 (January 1978): 122.

11. Bonnie Steinbock, "Speciesism and the Idea of Equality," *Philosophy* 53 (April 1978): 250.

12. See Lawrence Haworth, "Rights, Wrongs, and Animals," *Ethics* 88 (January 1978): 99.

13. Singer, *Animal Liberation*, pp. 172–73, and 160–63. Michael Fox, "Animal Liberation: A Critique," *Ethics* 88 (January 1978): 109, notices that for Singer the prohibition against killing animals is due to the *practical* impossibility in modern agribusiness to treat animals with consideration.

14. See Regan, "Moral Basis of Vegetarianism," p. 210. If one "must" eat meat (whatever that means), it is important to ask (à la Singer) *how* the animal was killed.

15. See Leonard Nelson, p. 153, in Godlovitch, Godlovitch, and Harris, eds., *Animals, Men, and Morals* (London: Taplinger, 1972). Also William H. Davis, "Man-Eating Aliens," *The Journal of Value Inquiry* 10 (Fall 1976): 179.

16. See Narveson, "Animal Rights," p. 166.

17. Fox, "Animal Liberation: A Critique," p. 110. The degree to which animals are similar to human beings with respect to suffering is treated by Singer, *Animal Liberation*, p. 49, where he points to the animal researcher's dilemma: either the animal is not like us, in which case there is no reason for performing the experiment, or the animal is like us, in which case we ought not to perform an experiment on the animal which would be considered outrageous if performed on one of us.

18. Cited in Singer, *Animal Liberation*, pp. 171–72.

19. I am not assuming a necessary connection between intelligence and feeling; I am only searching for Rorty's criteria for the attribution of feeling.

20. Even on an imaginative level Rorty's account seems defective; note the popularity of the cartoon character Porky Pig, or of Miss Piggy, who talk incessantly.

21. Singer, *Animal Liberation*, p. 188.

22. I am relying here on the work of Bernard Rollin and Peter Singer. See Rollin's "Beasts and Men: The Scope of Moral Concern," *Modern Schoolman* 55 (March, 1978).

23. See Robert S. Brumbaugh, "Man, Animals, and Morals: A Brief History," pp. 20–25, in Richard Knowles Morris, ed., *On the Fifth Day*.

24. Ibid., p. 24.

25. Hartshorne has written extensively since 1970 on animals, both as a metaphysician and as an expert on bird song. The following works will be mentioned; abbreviations follow: *Creative Synthesis and Philosophic Method* (La Salle, Ill.: Open Court, 1970)—CS; "Can Man Transcend His Animality?," *Monist* 55 (1971): 208–17—CM; "The Environmental Results of Technology," in *Philosophy and Environmental Crisis*, ed. William T. Blackstone (Athens, Ga.: University of Georgia Press, 1974), pp. 69–78—ER; "Foundations for a Humane Ethics: What Human Beings Have in Common with Other Higher Animals," in *On the Fifth Day*, ed. Richard Knowles Morris, pp. 154–72—FH; "The Rights of the Subhuman World," *Environmental Ethics* 1 (1979): 49–60—RS; "In Defense of Wordsworth's View of Nature," *Philosophy and Literature* 4 (1980): 80–91—DW; "The Ethics of Contributionism," in *Responsibilities to Future Generations: Environmental Ethics*, ed. Ernest Partridge (Buffalo: Prometheus Books, 1981), pp. 103–7—EC. It must be noted that Hartshorne never gives an ar-

gument for vegetarianism, although he does intimate the strengths he sees in the position. See FH, 162, 167, 170; RS, 49, 51, 54, 56, 58.

26. Immanuel Kant, *Lectures on Ethics*, trans. Louis Infield (New York: Harper and Row, 1963), pp. 239–40.

27. Also on the relationship between process philosophy and animals, see Susan B. Armstrong, *The Rights of Nonhuman Beings: A Whiteheadian Study* (Ph.D. diss., Bryn Mawr College, 1976), and John B. Bennett, "Ecology and Philosophy: Whitehead's Contribution," *Journal of Thought* 10 (1975): 24–30.

BIBLIOGRAPHY

A Ancient Sources

Aetna. Robinson Ellis, ed. Oxford: Oxford University Press, 1901.

Aratus. *Phaenomena.* Translated by G. R. Mair. Loeb ed., 1921.

Aristophanes. *Clouds.* Translated by B. B. Rogers. Loeb ed., 1927.

Aristotle. *Aristoteles Opera.* Edited by I. Bekker. Berlin, 1831; *The Works of Aristotle.* Translated under the editorship of W. D. Ross. Oxford: Clarendon Press, 1928.

Cicero. *De natura deorum.* Translated by H. Rackham. Loeb ed., 1933. *De officiis.* Translated by Walter Miller. Loeb ed., 1921; *Tusculanae disputationes.* Translated by J. E. King. Loeb ed., 1927.

Diodorus Siculus. *Bibliotheca historica.* Translated by C. H. Oldfather. Loeb ed., 1933.

Diogenes Laertius. *Lives of Eminent Philosophers.* Greek with English translation by R. D. Hicks. New York: Putnam, 1925.

Empedocles. *Die Fragmente der Vorsokratiker.* Edited by Hermann Diels, 1922; *Empedocles: The Extant Fragments.* Edited by M. R. Wright. New Haven: Yale University Press, 1981.

Epictetus. *Enchiridion.* Translated by W. A. Oldfather. Loeb ed., 1928.

Euripides. *Cresphontes.* In F. G. Welcker. *Die Griechischen Tragödien.* Bonn, 1841.

Herodotus. *Histories.* Translated by A. D. Godley. Loeb ed., 1926.

Hesiod. *Works and Days.* Edited by T. A. Sinclair. New York: Arno Press, 1979; *The Poems of Hesiod.* Translated by R. M. Frazer. Norman: University of Oklahoma Press, 1966.

Homer. *Iliad*. Translated by A. T. Murray. Loeb ed., 1924; *Odyssey*. Translated by A. T. Murray. Loeb ed., 1926.

Iamblichus. *De Vita Pythagorica*. Edited by L. Deubner. Leipzig, 1937; *Life of Pythagoras*. Translated by Thomas Taylor. London: Valpy, 1818.

Lucretius. *De rerum natura*. Translated by W. H. D. Rouse. Loeb ed., 1924.

Ovid. *Metamorphoses*. Translated by F. J. Miller. Loeb ed., 1921.

Philolaus. *Die Fragmente der Vorsokratiker*. Edited by Hermann Diels, 1922; Kathleen Freeman, *The Pre-Socratic Philosophers*. Oxford: Basil Blackwell, 1946; and *Ancilla*. Cambridge: Harvard University Press, 1948—also for other pre-Socratics.

Philostratus. *Life of Apollonius of Tyana*. Translated by F. C. Conybeare. Loeb ed., 1948.

Plato. *Platonis Opera*. Edited by J. Burnet. Oxford: Oxford University Press, 1900; *The Collected Dialogues of Plato*. Edited by E. Hamilton and H. Cairns. Princeton University Press, 1973.

Pliny. *Natural History*. Translated by H. Rackham, W. Jones, and D. Eicholz. Loeb ed., 1938–1962.

Plotinus. *Enneads*. Edited by Emile Brehier. Paris, 1924–1938; *The Enneads*. Translated by Stephen MacKenna. New York: Pantheon Books.

Plutarch. *Moralia*. Translated by F. C. Babbitt. Loeb ed., 1927; *Plutarch's Morals*. Edited by W. H. Goodwin. Boston: Little, Brown and Co., 1870; *Essays*. Translated by F. Babbitt, H. Fowler, and W. Helmbold. Loeb ed., 1927; "Letter of Consolation to His Wife." Translated by L. R. Loomis. In *Plutarch: Selected Lives and Essays*. Translated by Bernadotte Perrin. Loeb ed., 1916.

Porphyry. *Porphyre de l'abstinence*. Greek with French translation by J. Bouffartigue and M. Patillon. Paris, 1977. 3 vols.; *On Abstinence from Animal Food*. Translated by Thomas Taylor. London: Centaur Press, 1965. *Opuscula*. Edited by A. Nauck. Leipzig, 1886; *Life of Pythagoras*. In *Heroes and Gods*. Edited by M. Hadas and M. Smith. New York: Harper and Row. *De vita Plotini*. Edited by A. Westermann. Paris, 1878; "Life of Plotinus." Translated by Stephen MacKenna. In *The Enneads*. New York: Pantheon Books.

Seneca. *Seneca, ad Lucilium Epistulae Morales*. Translated by R. M. Gummere. Loeb ed., 1917–1925.

Sextus Empiricus. *Against the Logicians*. Translated by R. G. Bury. Loeb ed., 1961.

Strabo. *Geography*. Translated by H. L. Jones. Loeb ed., 1917.

Theophrastus. *Enquiry into Plants* and *Causes of Plants*. Translated by Arthur Hort. Loeb ed., 1916.

Xenophon. *Memorabilia*. Translated by E. C. Marchant. Loeb ed., 1923; *Recollections of Socrates*. Translated by A. S. Benjamin. Indianapolis: Bobbs-Merrill, 1965.

B Secondary Sources

Arbesmann, Rudolph. "Fasting and Prophecy in Pagan and Christian Antiquity." *Traditio* 7 (1949): 1–71. Useful in distinguishing between Greco-Roman abstinence and biblical fasting.

Auxter, Thomas. "The Right Not to be Eaten." *Inquiry* 22 (1979): 221–30. The current debate has focused too much attention on the concept of rights; defends a teleological theory of animal rights.

Balme, D. M. "Aristotle's Use of Differentiae in Zoology." In *Articles on Aristotle*, edited by J. Barnes, M. Schofield, and R. Sorabji. Vol. 1. London: Duckworth, 1975. Aristotle's intent in the *History of Animals* is not to classify animals, but just to study the differences among animals.

Barrow, R. H. *Plutarch and His Times*, pp. 112–18. London: Chatto and Windus, 1967. Deals with Plutarch's attitude toward animals, which the author claims may be the most sympathetic of any Greek writer.

Benson, John. "Duty and the Beast." *Philosophy* 53 (1978): 529–49. Assesses the work of Singer and Clark favorably, but these writers have only begun to deal with issues regarding animals.

Berman, Louis. *Vegetarianism and the Jewish Tradition.* Ktav Publishers, 1982. Argues for an underlying tendency toward vegetarianism within the biblical tradition.

Boas, George. "Theriophily." *Dictionary of the History of Ideas.* 1973. Vol. 4, pp. 384–88. A word coined by the author which refers to the expression of admiration for the character of animals: Diogenes and Plutarch are treated.

Bouffartigue, J., and Patillon, M., eds. *Porphyre de l'abstinence.* Paris, 1977. 3 vols. Helpful introductions and notes regarding Greek vegetarianism.

Boyd, M. J. "*De abstinentia* I, 7–12." *Classical Quarterly* (1936): 188–91. Deals with Porphyry's account of the Epicureans.

Broadie, A., and Pybus, Elizabeth M. "Kant's Treatment of Animals." *Philosophy* 49 (1974): 375–83. Show that Kant's position is that we cannot have direct duties to animals, but we can have "indirect" duties.

———. "Kant and the Maltreatment of Animals." *Philosophy* 53 (1978): 560–61. A point is clarified in response to Regan.

Brumbaugh, Robert S. "Man, Animals, and Morals: A Brief History." In *On the Fifth Day*, edited by Richard Knowles Morris. Just that, a brief history, with helpful treatments of the theory of evolution.

Burch, Robert W. "Animals, Rights, and Claims." *Southwestern Journal of Philosophy* 8 (1977): 53–59. Animals do not have rights because they lack moral agency, a capacity for moral self-defense, or a first-person orientation.

Callicott, J. Baird. "Animal Liberation: A Triangular Affair." *Environmental Ethics* 2 (1980): 311–38. Animal liberation is compared to the "land ethic" of Aldo Leopold, which includes plants, soils, and waters; i.e., pain is not the only moral evil.

Cave, George. "On the Irreplaceability of Animal Life." *Ethics and Animals* 3 (1982): 106–16. Argues against the replaceability argument; treats the conditions under which we can morally inflict pain on animals.

———. "Animals, Heidegger, and the Right to Life." *Environmental Ethics* 4 (1982): 249–54. Care is the essence of nonhuman animal as well as human *dasein*.

Cebik, L. B. "Can Animals Have Rights: No and Yes." *Philosophical Forum* (Boston) 12 (1981): 251–68. Animals may have legal rights, but not the moral rights alleged in the argument from marginal cases.

Cesaresco, Evelyn Martinengo. "The Greek Conception of Animals." *Contemporary Review* 85 (1904): 430–39. Good treatment of the Homeric Greeks, the Orphics, and Aesop.

———. "Animals at Rome." *Contemporary Review* 86 (1904): 225–34. Describes the circus, the gladitorial fights, pets, etc.

Cigman, Ruth. "Death, Misfortune, and Species Inequality." *Philosophy and Public Affairs* 10 (1981). Holds that only beings capable of valuing life itself can suffer the misfortune of death; therefore animals cannot have a right to life.

Clark, Stephen R. L. *The Moral Status of Animals* (Oxford: Clarendon Press, 1977). A defense of vegetarianism by a Christian Neoplatonist. Syncretistic, relying on: the sentience of animals, the absence of an absolute dichotomy between man and beast, the abhorrence of the "might makes right" attitude. Attempts to place ethics, epistemology, and man into their proper environmental setting, acknowledging a community not merely of races and cultures, but also of species.

———. "Animal Wrongs." *Analysis* 38 (1978): 147–49. Argues against Frey by suggesting that mistreating imbeciles is, in moral terms, the very same wrong as mistreating chimps.

———. *The Nature of the Beast: Are Animals Moral?* Oxford: Oxford University Press, 1982. Studies the philosophical implications of animal intelligence, altruism, sexuality, and community.

Cottingham, John. "'A Brute to the Brutes?': Descartes' Treatment of Animals." *Philosophy* 53 (1978): 551–59. Descartes does not hold the monstrous view of animals that some suggest; however, his position regarding animals is by no means clear.

Davis, William H. "Man-Eating Aliens." *The Journal of Value Inquiry* 10 (1976): 178–85. Constructs a thought experiment in which a race of aliens invades our planet, intending to use us for food; considers three grounds of appeal we could make to them.

Dawkins, Marian Stamp. *Animal Suffering: The Science of Animal Welfare.* London: Chapman and Hall, 1980. There is no single argument to tell us if, and to what extent, animals suffer; a synthesis of several methods is used.

Detienne, M. "La Cuisine de Pythagore." *Archives de Sociologie des Religions* 29 (1970): 141–62. The question of what the Pythagoreans ate is of prime importance: if they were vegetarians they were primarily a religious sect; if not, they were more of a political movement.

————. "Entre bêtes et Dieux." *Nouvelle Revue de Psychanalyse* IV (1972): 230–46. The myth of the golden age exhibits a desire for transcendence, which in its upward direction can lead to vegetarianism, but in its downward, bestial direction it can lead to anthropophagy.

Devine, Philip E. "The Moral Basis of Vegetarianism." *Philosophy* 53 (1978): 481–505. Although this is an attack on vegetarianism (especially Singer's), an intermediate position between vegetarianism and conventional eating of animals is developed.

Diamond, Cora. "Eating Meat and Eating People." *Philosophy* 53 (1978): 465–79. Argues against Singer and Regan, whose appeal to the prevention of suffering encourages us to neglect animals as fellow creatures; a non-utilitarian approach to vegetarianism.

Dierauer, U. *Tier und Mensch im Denken der Antike*. Amsterdam, 1977, 286–90. Distinguishes two types of ancient vegetarianism: (1) that which wants to spare animals; and (2) that which is concerned with the soul of man.

Dombrowski, Daniel A. "Rorty on Pre-Linguistic Awareness in Pigs." *Ethics & Animals* 4 (1983): 2–5. Rorty's treatment of nonhuman animals is not sufficient to establish the case for meat-eating, as Rorty seems to think.

————. "Eating and Spiritual Exercises: Food for Thought from St. Ignatius and Nikos Kazantzakis." *Christianity and Literature*, forthcoming, 1983. Studies how eating plays an essential role in these two writers' theological positions.

————. "Was Plato a Vegetarian?" To appear in *Apeiron*, forthcoming, 1984. Argues that it is unfortunate that this question has seldom been asked; there are not sufficient grounds to conclude that Plato was opposed to vegetarianism.

————. "Vegetarianism and the Argument from Marginal Cases in Porphyry." *Journal of the History of Ideas*, forthcoming, 1984. Porphyry's status as the discoverer of the argument from marginal cases ought to be acknowledged.

Donaghy, Kevin. "Singer on Speciesism." *Philosophic Exchange* (1974). Argues that what entitles human beings to a privileged position in the moral community is a certain minimal level of intelligence.

Etyka 18 (1980). Several articles on animal rights in Polish; many are reprints of articles by English-speaking philosophers.

Fowler, Corbin. "Freedom: Animal Rights, Human Rights, and Superhuman Rights." *Auslegung* 4 (1976): 52–63. Compares human treatment of animals with possible superhuman treatment of humans.

Fox, Michael. "Animal Liberation: A Critique." *Ethics* 88 (1978): 106–18. Although the infliction of unnecessary suffering on animals is a matter of concern, Singer and Regan have not made the case for animals' rights nor for their condemnation of speciesism.

————. "Animal Suffering and Rights." *Ethics* 88 (1978): 134–38. Having the capacity to suffer and enjoy is a necessary but not sufficient condition for having rights, which would have to include autonomy.

Fox, Michael W. *Returning to Eden: Animal Rights and Human Responsibility* (New York: Viking Press, 1980). A popular endorsement of a "biospiritual" ethic based on our kinship with the rest of creation.

Francis, Leslie Pickering, and Norman, Richard. "Some Animals are More Equal than Others." *Philosophy* 53 (1978): 507–27. Criticism of Singer; an argument for attaching greater weight to the interests of human beings than animals because of the former's communicative, economic, political, and familial relationships.

Frey, R. G. "Animal Rights." *Analysis* 37 (1977): 186–89. Criticizes the argument from marginal cases.

————. "Interests and Animal Rights." *Philosophical Quarterly* 27 (1977): 254–59. Argues against Regan that the analysis of what it is to have interests makes no essential reference to the existence of other or of competent people.

————. *Interests and Rights: The Case against Animals.* Oxford: Clarendon Press, 1980. An analysis of what it means to have interests. Reaches the conclusion that animals do not have these, hence they do not have rights. Criticizes converters like Singer who do not foster a critical attitude in the application of philosophy to practical issues. A general attack on moral rights, even human ones.

Giehl, Dudley. *Vegetarianism: A Way of Life.* New York: Harper and Row, 1981. General survey of the ethical, ecological, economic, and health considerations of vegetarianism.

Gill, James E. "Theriophily in Antiquity: A Supplementary Account." *Journal of the History of Ideas* 30 (1969): 401–12. Supplements the work of Lovejoy and Boas on theriophily, the position that animals are in some way superior to men; examines Aristotle, Cynics, Stoics, and Plutarch.

Godlovitch, Roslind. "Animals and Morals." *Philosophy* 46 (January 1971): 23–33. Argues that there is no a priori reason to deny that animals can have moral rights; animals have the right not to suffer but do not have the right to live.

Godlovitch, Stanley; Godlovitch, Roslind; and Harris, John, eds. *Animals, Men, and Morals.* London: Taplinger, 1972. Contains selections from various authors; three deal with the moral framework: Leonard Nelson (on duties to animals); Roslind Godlovitch (on weak and strong duties to animals); and Stanley Godlovitch (on animals as utilities—the author holds that animals are ends in themselves).

Goodpaster, K., and Sayre, K., eds. *Ethics and Problems of the 21st Century*. South Bend: University of Notre Dame Press, 1979. A collection of philosophical essays, including those by Frankena (who distinguishes six classes of moral theories, some of which concern animals); R. and V. Routley (who seek alternatives to "humans only" morality); and Singer.

Gorman, Peter. *Pythagoras: A Life*. London: Routledge and Kegan Paul, 1978. A biography which at several points treats the issue of vegetarianism in Pythagoras and his followers.

Grant, Robert. "Dietary Laws Among Pythagoreans, Jews, and Christians." *Harvard Theological Review* 73 (1980): 299–310. Explores the "allegorical method" in relation to dietary laws in these groups.

Gunn, Alastair. "Traditional Ethics and the Moral Status of Animals." *Environmental Ethics* 5 (1983): 133–53. Utilitarianism and rights theory are historically and logically tied to individualism, which is incapable of understanding the moral status of animals; "stewardship" is a more appropriate concept.

Hartshorne, Charles. *Creative Synthesis and Philosophic Method*. LaSalle, Ill.: Open Court, 1970. A major work in process metaphysics which has profound implications for our dealings with animals.

———. "Can Man Transcend His Animality?" *Monist* 55 (1971): 208–17. In facing the concrete, man is never more than a thinking animal; in his abstract thought he entertains superanimal ideals.

———. "The Environmental Results of Technology." In *Philosophy and Environmental Crisis*, edited by William T. Blackstone. Athens, Ga.: University of Georgia Press, 1974. Man is the freest creature, hence the most dangerous to himself and other animals.

———. "Foundations for a Humane Ethics: What Human Beings Have in Common with Other Higher Animals." In *On the Fifth Day*, edited by Richard Knowles Morris. Explores the ethical implications of the cell theory and the presence of nervous systems in vertebrates.

———. "The Rights of the Subhuman World." *Environmental Ethics* 1 (1979): 49–60. Distinguishes among legal, moral, and ethical rights; animals have intrinsic as well as instrumental value.

———. "In Defense of Wordsworth's View of Nature." *Philosophy and Literature* 4 (1980): 80–91. Twentieth-century science forces us to take Wordsworth and his view of animals seriously again.

———. "The Ethics of Contributionism." In *Responsibilities to Future Generations: Environmental Ethics*, edited by Ernest Partridge. Buffalo: Prometheus Books, 1981. Our most inclusive obligation is to optimize our gifts to the future, including our present happiness.

Hasker, William. "The Souls of Beasts and Men." *Religious Studies* 10 (1974): 265–77. Presents an "emergentist," nondualistic ontology which is consistent with religious affirmations about personal survival.

Haussleiter, Johannes. *Der Vegetarismus in der antike*. Berlin: Topelmann, 1935. The only extended treatment previous to this book on ancient vegetarianism. See chapter 1 where I discuss Haussleiter.

Haworth, Lawrence. "Rights, Wrongs, and Animals." *Ethics* 88 (1978): 95–105. Suggests that X has a right over Y to do Z if and only if: (1) X's doing Z is not wrong; and (2) Y's interference with X's doing Z injures X. The scope of X includes some animals.

Hoff, Christina. "Kant's Invidious Humanism." *Environmental Ethics* 5 (1983): 63–70. Kant's rational humanism is arbitrary and morally impoverished; analyzes the move to the second formulation of the categorical imperative.

Huby, Pamela M. "The Epicureans, Animals and Freewill." *Apeiron* 3 (1969): 17–19. Deals with a difference in Lucretius and Epicurus: the former attributes free will to (tame) animals whereas the latter denies it to (wild) animals.

Hughes, J. Donald. "Ecology in Ancient Greece." *Inquiry* 18 (1975): 115–25. The Greeks displayed two major attitudes toward nature: it was both the theater of the gods and the theater of reason. The latter attitude yielded Aristotle and Theophrastus.

———. "The Environmental Ethics of the Pythagoreans." *Environmental Ethics* 3 (1980): 195–213. Two conflicting tendencies can be found in Pythagorean ethics: (1) a sense of reverence for animals and nature; and (2) a doctrine of separability of soul and body which denigrates nature.

Husak, Douglas. "On the Rights of Non-Persons." *Canadian Journal of Philosophy* 10 (1980): 607–22. Discusses two fallacies of arguments that say nonpersons have moral rights.

Jamieson, Dale. "Rational Egoism and Animal Rights." *Environmental Ethics* 3 (1981): 167–71. Argues that rational egoism provides only a principled indifference to the fate of animals, contra Narveson.

Jamieson, Dale, and Regan, Tom. "Animal Rights: A Reply to Frey." *Analysis* 38 (1978): 32–36. Frey does not show that the arguments of the "animal rightists" fail; nor, if they do fail, why.

Jones, Gary E., and Perry, Clifton. "On Animal Rights." *Applied Philosophy* 1 (1982): 39–57.

Jones, Hardy. "Reply: Concerning the Moral Status of Animals." *Southwestern Journal of Philosophy* 8 (1977): 61–63. Reply to Burch's denial of animal rights.

Jung, Hwa Yol. "The Orphic Voice and Ecology." *Environmental Ethics* 3 (1981): 329–40. A plea to return to the Orphic voice as the sound basis for developing an ecological ethic; music and poetry are emphasized.

Kushner, Thomasine. "Interpretations of 'Life' and Prohibitions Against Killing." *Environmental Ethics* 3 (1981): 147–54. Explores the ambiguous term "life" from both an Eastern and Western perspective so as to develop rules against killing.

Lamb, David. "Animal Rights and Liberation Movements." *Environmental Ethics* 4 (1982): 215–33. Contra Singer, only reform movements are possible for animals, not liberation movements.

Levin, Michael E. "Animal Rights Evaluated." *Humanist* 37 (1977). By all the "usual criteria" animals have no rights: voluntary consent, rationality, etc.

———. "All in a Stew About Animals: A Reply to Singer." *Humanist* 37 (1977). Accuses Singer of "demagogic hyperbole," among other things, and says vegetarianism would wreck the world's economy.

Linzey, Andrew. *Animal Rights: A Christian Assessment of Man's Treatment of Animals.* London: SCM Press, 1976. Argues for animal rights on theological and philosophical grounds; treats Albert Schweitzer's concept of reverence for life.

Lloyd, G. E. R. "The Development of Aristotle's Theory of the Classification of Animals." *Phronesis* 6 (1961): 59–81. Traces the development in non-biological and biological works; in both, Aristotle starts out using the Platonic method of division, then criticizes this method in favor of a more empirical one; but teleology is found even in Aristotle's late classifications.

Lloyd, Genevieve. "Spinoza's Environmental Ethics." *Inquiry* 23 (1980): 293–311. Develops possible responses to Spinoza's rejection of animal rights.

Lockwood, Michael. "Singer on Killing and the Preference for Life." *Inquiry* 22 (1979): 157–70. Holds that Singer's position (i.e., that the killing of "lower" animals, infants, etc., is not directly wrong if loss of happiness is made good by the creation of new sentient life) is inadequate.

Lonsdale, Steven H. "Attitudes toward Animals in Ancient Greece." *Greece and Rome* 26 (1979): 146–59. Wideranging study that concludes that man's relationship with animals was neither simply one of superiority or submission.

Lovejoy, Arthur, and Boas, George. *Primitivism and Related Ideas in Antiquity.* New York: Octagon Books, 1965. Because vegetarianism was associated with the golden age, it is one of the "primitive" ideas studied, along with anthropophagy, etc.

Lowry, Jon W. "Natural Rights: Men and Animals." *Southwestern Journal of Philosophy* 6 (1975): 109–22. Natural rights can be understood as necessary conditions for the achievement of the aim of an entity; these can be applicable to creatures other than man.

McCloskey, H. J. "Rights." *Philosophical Quarterly* 15 (1965): 115–27. Excludes animals as possible possessors of rights because: (1) they cannot possess things; and (2) they do not have interests, and only beings that have interests can have rights.

———. "The Right to Life." *Mind* 84 (1975): 410–13. Although good reasons are required to kill sentient animals, this is not tantamount to, and does not entail, that animals have rights.

———. "Moral Rights and Animals." *Inquiry* 22 (1979): 23–54. Holds that only beings that possess (actually or potentially) the capacity for moral self-determination can be possessors of rights; explores the rights animals could possess *if* they possessed rights.

McGinn, Colin. "Evolution, Animals, and the Basis of Morality." *Inquiry* 22 (1979): 81–99. Claims that morality is a necessary corollary of advanced intelligence, which includes nonhuman animals.

Magel, Charles. *A Bibliography on Animal Rights and Related Matters.* Washington, D.C.: University Press of America, 1981. The best bibliography available.

Magel, Charles, and Regan, Tom. "Animal Rights and Human Obligations: A Select Bibliography." *Inquiry* 22 (1979): 243–47. Shorter than above.

Malcolm, Norman. "Thoughtless Brutes." In *Thought and Knowledge*, pp. 40–57. Ithaca: Cornell University Press, 1977. Holds that the relationship between language and thought must be so close that it is really senseless to conjecture that animals have thoughts; they may "think that p" but they cannot "have the thought that p."

Margolis, Joseph. "Animals Have No Rights and Are Not the Equal of Humans." *Philosophic Exchange* 1 (1974): 119–23. Criticizes Singer's position by holding that where it is compelling it is trivial, and where it is not trivial it is not compelling; it is hopeless to ascribe certain rights to animals.

Martin, Michael W. "A Critique of Moral Vegetarianism." *Reason Papers* (1976). It has yet to be shown that there is a moral obligation not to eat meat in our society.

Matthews, Gareth B. "Animals and the Unity of Psychology." *Philosophy* 53 (1978): 437–54. Argues in favor of the Principle of Psychological Continuity, which suggests that psychological acts in lower animals model those in higher animals. This principle was held by Plato and Aristotle, opposed by Descartes and Malcolm.

Morris, Richard Knowles, ed. *On the Fifth Day: Animal Rights and Human Ethics.* Washington, D.C.: Acropolis Press, 1978. Contains essays by Brumbaugh and Hartshorne (see separate entries) as well as by Joel Feinberg (on animal rights), John B. Cobb (on anthropocentrism), and F. S. C. Northrop (on animate compassion).

Morsink, Johannes. *Aristotle on the Generation of Animals.* Washington, D.C.: University Press of America, 1982. Aristotle is much less of a Baconian than many suppose; sees Aristotle making Popperian conjectures and refutations.

Naess, Arne. "Environmental Ethics and Spinoza's Ethics." *Inquiry* 23 (1980): 313–25. Spinoza's philosophy is a source of inspiration to environmentalists, even if he was a speciesist.

Narveson, Jan. "Animal Rights." *Canadian Journal of Philosophy* 7 (1977): 161–78. Claims that egoism gives a coherent account of our moral intuitions regarding the legitimate eating of animals, as does utilitarianism (contra Singer and Regan).

Nielson, Kai. "Persons, Morals and the Animal Kingdom." *Man and World* 11 (1978): 231–56. There are no grounds for our "humanocentric" attitudes toward animals, and it is our duty to avoid causing unnecessary suffering.

Nozick, Robert. *Anarchy, State, and Utopia,* pp. 35–47. New York: Basic Books, 1974. Tries to determine what justifies moral side constraints and analyzes the double standard of the dictum, "utilitarianism for animals, Kantianism for people."

Passmore, John. *Man's Responsibility for Nature.* London: Duckworth, 1974. Animals do not form a moral community because such a community requires mutual obligations and common interests; rights are not applicable to nonhumans.

———. "The Treatment of Animals." *Journal of the History of Ideas* 36 (1975): 195–218. A historical tracing of the process by which Western man has divested himself of certain rights to treat animals as he pleases, but not to the point so as to limit man's domination of the world.

Paterson, David, and Ryder, Richard, eds. *Animals' Rights: A Symposium.* London: Centaur Press, 1979. Collection of essays, including those by Regan, Sprigge, Clark, Frey, and Duffy.

Perry, Clifton. "We Are What We Eat." *Environmental Ethics* (1981): 341–50. Argues against eating animals when some people in the world are starving, and offers other suggestions to avoid immoral waste.

Pierce, Christine. "Can Animals be Liberated?" *Philosophical Studies* 36 (1979): 69–75. Although humans do not deserve moral consideration because they are human, Singer's revelation of speciesism does not support a liberation of animals parallel to liberation of women and blacks.

Pluhar, Evelyn B. "Must an Opponent of Animal Rights Also Be an Opponent of Human Rights?" *Inquiry* 24 (1981): 229–41. Criticizes what is usually called the argument from marginal cases, or, as Pluhar puts it, nonparadigmatic humans.

———. "On Replaceability." *Ethics & Animals* 3 (1982): 96–105. Argues against Singer's replaceability argument; favors Regan's inherent value stance; treats self-consciousness in animals.

Povilitis, Anthony J. "On Assigning Rights to Animals and Nature." *Environmental Ethics* 2 (1980): 67–71. Criticizes Watson's "reciprocity framework" as being too anthropomorphic, and as incorrectly equating moral rights with "primary rights"; also, the golden rule is incorrectly interpreted by Watson.

Pritchard, Michael S., and Robison, Wade L. "Justice and the Treatment of Animals: A Critique of Rawls." *Environmental Ethics* 3 (1981): 55–61. Because animals are not participants in Rawls's original position, it is possible that the principles adopted would conflict with what Rawls calls duties of compassion and humanity toward animals.

Quarelli, Elena. *Socrates and the Animals*. Translated by K. Speight. London: Hodder and Stoughton, 1960. A work by an Italian philosopher-poet that tries to establish (in Socratic fashion) that animals have incorporeal, immortal souls; relies on the *Phaedo*.

Rachels, James. "Vegetarianism and 'The Other Weight Problem'." In *World Hunger and Moral Obligation*, edited by W. Aiken and H. LaFollette. Englewood Cliffs, N.J.: Prentice-Hall, 1977. Argues that the inefficiency of raising animals for the table deprives the starving of the world of grain that could otherwise be available for human consumption.

Reeve, E. Gavin. "Speciesism and Equality." *Philosophy* 53 (1978): 562–63. A moving example is cited to support the thesis that animals have certain minimal conceptual abilities for having rights.

Regan, Tom. "The Moral Basis of Vegetarianism." *Canadian Journal of Philosophy* 5 (1975): 181–214. Argues for "conditional vegetarianism": unless one can show how the undeserved, nontrivial pain and killing animals experience is not gratuitous and does not violate the rights of animals, then the vegetarian is justified; puts the onus of justification on the meat eater.

———. "Broadie and Pybus on Kant." *Philosophy* 51 (1976): 471–72. A minor disagreement with Broadie and Pybus.

———. "McCloskey on Why Animals Cannot Have Rights." *Philosophical Quarterly* 26 (1976): 251–57. McCloskey fails to show that there is any logical abnormality involved in speaking of what is in the interests of animals. Interests-1 (things a being is interested in) are distinct from interests-2 (when A has an interest in X means X would benefit A).

———. "Feinberg on What Sorts of Beings Can Have Rights." *Southern Journal of Philosophy* (1976): 485–97. Criticizes Feinberg's contention that plants and mere things cannot have rights.

———. "Frey on Interests and Animal Rights." *Philosophical Quarterly* 27 (1977): 335–37. There being other competent persons about is necessary *if* speaking of what is in the animal's interests is to have *prescriptive* meaning.

———. "Narveson on Rational Egoism and the Rights of Animals." *Canadian Journal of Philosophy* 7 (1977): 179–86. Argues that Narveson's rational egoism could sanction our treating some morons in flagrantly immoral ways, thereby showing the inadequacy of his position on animals.

———. "Fox's Critique of Animal Liberation." *Ethics* 88 (1978): 126–33. Criticizes Fox by suggesting that if an animal has characteristics a, b, c . . . n but lacks autonomy, then we have as much reason to believe that the animal has rights as the human.

———. "An Examination and Defense of One Argument Concerning Animal Rights." *Inquiry* 22 (1979): 189–219. Basic moral rights ought to be extended to animals because of the notion of inherent value, which also supports the rights of infants and the severely mentally enfeebled.

———. "Animal Rights, Human Wrongs." *Environmental Ethics* 2 (1980): 99–120. Shows the inadequacy of three accounts of our duties toward animals: (1) the Kantian position; (2) the cruelty account; and (3) the utilitarian position, e.g., Singer's position.

———. "Cruelty, Kindness, and Unnecessary Suffering." *Philosophy* 55 (1980): 532–41. Our duties to animals cannot be reduced to the avoidance of cruelty and the practice of kindness, because these involve references to the mind of the agent; "unnecessary suffering" must be considered.

———. "Utilitarianism, Vegetarianism, and Animal Rights." *Philosophy and Public Affairs* 9 (1980): 305–24. Disputes Singer's claim that the obligations of vegetarianism are based on the principle of utility.

———. "On the Right Not to be Made to Suffer Gratuitously." *Canadian Journal of Philosophy* 10 (1980): 473–78. A reply to Vandeveer on the issue of unnecessary animal suffering.

———. "Utilitarianism and Vegetarianism Again." *Ethics & Animals* 2 (1981): 2–7. Raises new challenges to Singer's position.

———. "The Nature and Possibility of an Environmental Ethic." *Environmental Ethics* (1981). Embraces the idea that nonsentient beings, such as trees and rivers, can have moral rights.

———. *All That Dwell Therein: Essays on Animal Rights and Environmental Ethics.* Berkeley: University of California Press, 1982. A collection of some of Regan's essays, in which he develops his thesis that all or some animals may qualify as rights holders, based not on equal consideration of interests or sentience but on the criterion of "inherent value."

Regan, Tom, and Singer, Peter, eds. *Animal Rights and Human Obligations.* Englewood Cliffs, N.J.: Prentice-Hall, 1976. A wideranging set of readings in three categories: (1) historical—Bible, Aristotle, Plutarch, Aquinas, Descartes, Montaigne, Voltaire, Hume, Kant, Schopenhauer, Bentham, Mill, Darwin; (2) more recent selections published previously—Salt, Ritchie, Rickaby, Regan, Singer, Midgley, Feinberg; and (3) original essays—Rachels, Vandeveer.

Richards, Stewart. "Forethoughts for Carnivores." *Philosophy* 56 (1981): 73–87. Written by a philosopher-zoologist who argues that it is prima facie wrong to be cruel to animals; defends vegetarianism.

Rodman, John. "The Other Side of Ecology in Ancient Greece: Comments on Hughes." *Inquiry* 19 (1976): 108–12. The classical roots of ecological sensibility lie not only in the theater of reason but in the theater of the gods, exemplified in Pythagoras and Empedocles.

———. "The Liberation of Nature?" *Inquiry* 20 (1977): 83–131. Agrees in large part with Singer, but would go further than the sentiency criterion so as to include natural objects within the sphere of moral concern; criticizes Singer's liberation analogy.

————. "Animal Justice: The Counter-Revolution in Natural Right and Law." *Inquiry* 22 (1979): 3–22. Deals with the notion of *jus natural* in the Roman jurists, who defined it in terms of what nature had taught all animals; and Grotius, whose revolution in the concept excluded nonhuman animals.

Rollin, Bernard E. "Beasts and Men: The Scope of Moral Concern." *Modern Schoolman* 55 (1978): 241–60. Criticizes the Kantian argument that rationality-language is the sufficient condition for a being to be the object of moral concern.

————. *Animal Rights and Human Morality.* Buffalo: Prometheus Books, 1981. A development of a theory of animal rights by an author who also knows biology; deals with moral and legal issues, animal research, and pets.

Rorty, Richard. *Philosophy and the Mirror of Nature.* Princeton: Princeton University Press, 1979. On prelinguistic awareness in animals; see chapter 7, where I treat Rorty.

Rosenfield, Leonora. *From Beast-Machine to Man-Machine.* New York: Octagon Books, 1968. Deals with animal soul in French thought from Descartes to the Aristotelian and Neoplatonic anti-Cartesians, to the Epicurean empiricists.

Salt, Henry S. *Animals' Rights.* Clarks Summit, Pa.: Society for Animal Rights, 1980. New edition of this late nineteenth-century classic with a preface by Singer and a bibliography by Magel.

Sapontzis, S. F. "Are Animals Moral Beings?" *American Philosophical Quarterly* 17 (1980): 45–52. Argues that traditional positions that animals do not act morally because there is a necessary condition to morality in reason are fallacious; consequently, animals merit moral respect.

————. "Must We Value Life to Have a Right to It?" *Ethics & Animals* 3 (1982): 2–11. Argues against Cigman that having a right to X does not require that we value X; further, the right to life is a part of the right not to suffer, in that life is essential to avoid suffering.

————. "On Being Morally Expendable." *Ethics & Animals* 3 (1982): 58–72. Examines the replaceability argument from the perspective of autonomy-based views and from utilitarian perspectives.

————. "The Moral Significance of Interests." *Environmental Ethics* 4 (1982): 345–58. The epistemic differences between human and animal interests are not morally significant.

Scarborough, John. "Beans, Pythagoras, Taboos, and Ancient Dietetics." *Classical World* 75 (1982): 355–58. Cites the many studies of favism, many of which suggest that the Pythagoreans' prohibition of beans was for medical reasons (e.g., Brumbaugh and Schwartz); the author sees other reasons at work as well.

Schöne, Hermann. "*De abstinentia* I, 34." *Rheinisches Museum für Philologie*

LXXIII: 443–48. Deals with the relationship between Porphyry's vegetarianism and medicine.

Seidler, Michael J. "Hume and the Animals." *Southern Journal of Philosophy*
15 (1977): 361–72. Hume was led to a consideration of animals by the skeptical tradition, his experimental method, and ethical considerations; but
human ethics does not extend to animals.

Sikora, R. I. "Morality and Animals." *Ethics & Animals* 2 (1981): 46–59. Attempts to rebut some of the more common objections to the animal liberation movement.

Singer, Peter. "Animal Liberation." *The New York Review of Books* (April 5,
1973). An early expression of Singer's views.

———. *Animal Liberation: A New Ethics for Our Treatment of Animals*. New
York: New York Review, 1975. Develops the notion of speciesism, modeled
after racism and sexism. The use of animals in research, factory farming,
vegetarianism, and a short history of speciesism are included. Singer's own
position is a utilitarian one.

———. "A Reply to Professor Levin's 'Animal Rights Evaluated'." *Humanist* 37
(1977). Emphasizes his utilitarian framework against Levin's misinterpreta-
tion.

———. "The Fable of the Fox and the Unliberated Animals." *Ethics* 88 (1978):
119–25. Rights are not essential to Singer's position, but equality is; refutes
the idea that autonomy is required to be a part of a moral community.

———. "Killing Humans and Killing Animals." *Inquiry* 22 (1979): 145–56. To
say that animals ought not to be made to suffer unnecessarily is not the
same as saying that they ought not to be killed. Other capacities must be
considered to make the latter claim, e.g., having a future.

———. *Practical Ethics*, chap. 5. Cambridge: Cambridge University Press, 1979.
Rejects some of the views held in *Animal Liberation* in favor of the replaceability argument, in which animals are replaceable receptacles for
value.

———. "Utilitarianism and Vegetarianism." *Philosophy and Public Affairs* 9
(1980): 325–37. Replies to the gaps found in *Animal Liberation*'s utilitarian argument.

———. "Animals and the Value of Life." In *Matters of Life and Death*, edited by
Tom Regan. Philadelphia: Temple University Press, 1980. An introduction
to various issues regarding animals; includes a critique of Regan. Develops
the replaceability argument that replacement provides adequate compen-
sation for painfully killing a sentient being.

Sprigge, T. L. S. "Metaphysics, Physicalism, and Animal Rights." *Inquiry* 22
(1979): 101–43. Cruelty to animals is built upon an ontology of animal reality, which may be a physicalist metaphysics, to be distinguished from
metaphysical naturalism.

Squadrito, Kathy. "Descartes, Locke, and the Soul of Animals." *Philosophy Re-*

search *Archives* 6 (1980). Locke does not attribute reason to beasts, and his position does not differ greatly from that of Descartes.

Steinbock, Bonnie. "Speciesism and the Idea of Equality." *Philosophy* 53 (1978): 247–56. Agrees with Singer that we are obliged to consider the interests of all sentient creatures, but the interests of animals are not equal to those of humans.

Stubbs, Anne C. "Morality and Our Treatment of Animals." *Philosophical Studies* (Ireland) 27 (1980): 29–39. Universalizability compels us to widen the traditional field of application of cruelty and exploitation.

Vandeveer, Donald. "Interspecific Justice." *Inquiry* 22 (1979): 55–79. Proposes a nonanthropocentric basis for discounting the interests of sentient animals and examines means of adjudicating interspecific conflicts of interest.

———. "Of Beasts, Persons, and the Original Position." *Monist* 62 (1979): 368–77. Questions whether the impartiality of Rawls's original position is due to the fact that its members must be human.

———. "Animal Suffering." *Canadian Journal of Philosophy* 10 (1980): 463–71. The expression "unnecessary suffering" is ambiguous and cannot be used straightforwardly to settle disputes about animals.

Vidal-Naquet, P. "Plato's Myth of the Statesman, the Ambiguities of the Golden Age and of History." *The Journal of Hellenic Studies* 98 (1978): 132–41. Treats the Greek myth of the golden age and its vegetarianism through various authors, especially Plato.

Watson, Richard A. "Self-Consciousness and the Rights of Nonhuman Animals and Nature." *Environmental Ethics* 1 (1979): 99–129. Living entities do not have intrinsic rights unless they are capable of fulfilling reciprocal duties in a self-conscious manner.

Wenz, Peter S. "Act-Utilitarianism and Animal Liberation." *Personalist* 60 (1979): 423–28. Arguments for animal liberation are only as strong as the ethical theory on which they are based; act utilitarian theory ordinarily requires people to obstruct animal liberation in our society.

White, James E. "Are Sentient Beings Replaceable?" *Ethics & Animals* 3 (1982): 91–95. Argues that Singer's replaceability argument fails.

Willard, L. Duane. "About Animals 'Having' Rights." *Journal of Value Inquiry* 16 (1982): 177–87. Both animals and humans "have" rights only in the sense that this reflects human decisions concerning how humans and animals ought to be treated.

Williams, Howard. *The Ethics of Diet*. London: Richard James, 1907. A biographical history of vegetarianism, including treatments of Hesiod, Pythagoras, Empedocles, Plato, Ovid, Seneca, Musonius, Plutarch, and Porphyry. Goes all the way to the nineteenth century.

Williams, Meredith. "Rights, Interests, and Moral Equality." *Environmental Ethics* 2 (1980): 149–61. Disagrees with Singer's claim that the interests of animals merit equal consideration with those of human beings.

Wynne-Tyson, E. "Introduction." In Porphyry, *On Abstinence from Animal Food*, translated by T. Taylor. London: Centaur Press, 1965. Helpful notes and introduction to this recent edition of Taylor's translation of Porphyry.

INDEX OF NAMES